Investment, Expectations and Uncertainty

INVESTMENT, EXPECTATIONS AND UNCERTAINTY

Ciaran Driver and David Moreton

BLACKWELL
Oxford UK & Cambridge USA

Copyright © Ciaran Driver and David Moreton 1992

The right of Ciaran Driver and David Moreton to be identified
as authors of this work has been asserted in accordance with the
Copyright, Designs and Patents Act 1988.

First published 1992

Blackwell Publishers
108 Cowley Road
Oxford OX4 1 JF
UK

Three Cambridge Center
Cambridge, Massachusetts 02142
USA

British Library Cataloguing in Publication Data

A CIP catalogue record for this book is available from the British Library.

Library of Congress Cataloging in Publication Data

Driver, Ciaran.
Investment, expectations and uncertainty/Ciaran Driver and David Moreton.
p.   cm.
Includes bibliographical references and index.
ISBN 0–631–17334–X (alk. paper)
1. Risk.   2. Uncertainty.   3. Investment-Decision making.
I. Moreton, David.   II. Title
HB615.D75   1992
332.6–dc20   91-27566   CIP

Typeset in 11 on 13 pt Times
by Colset Private Ltd., Singapore
Printed in Great Britain by T.J. Press, Padstow, Cornwall

This book is printed on acid-free paper.

A wisdom so tenderly precise, and so precisely circumspect, is a
mortal enemy to haughty executions.

Montaigne

The right use of bold persons is, that they never command in chief.

Bacon

Contents

Contents

Preface

Writing this book has been a lengthy, though enjoyable, process. The argument originated in a largely unsupported assertion in my previous book *Towards Full Employment* that economic activity was constrained by uncertainty induced by structural change. At that time I had only the evidence of a consultancy research paper I had written in 1986 commissioned by Michael Posner for the National Economic Development Office, and summarized in appendix 7.1. That skeleton evidence has now been fleshed out in this book and provided with a more substantive context.

The text of the book is my responsibility. The econometric work owes much to David Moreton, who worked on the material both during his time as project research assistant and later in the preparation of the material for publication. The assistance of the Economic and Social Research Council in providing funding is gratefully acknowledged. We are also grateful to Blackwell Publishers and to the editors of *The Economic Journal* for permission to include material from Driver and Moreton (1991) in Chapter 7.

It is a pleasure to record help from many sources. Karl Aiginger provided gentle but precise criticism of draft chapter 4 and more generally. Philip Arestis read and commented on most draft chapters. Drafts of individual chapters were read (sometimes in very early draft, so the usual disclaimer applies *a fortiori*) by Tony Buxton, Keith Cuthbertson, Tony Lawson, Anne Phillips, Malcolm Sawyer, Aubrey Silberston and Ron Smith. Vicky Chick kindly read the chapters in proof. Some data were kindly provided by Ken Holden; Chris Whitbread helped with the industry-level data. Mathematical advice was given by Jerry Coakley, Robin Hewins, Nigel Meade and Lynda White. Thanos Skouras sent the funniest non-comment. David Shepherd encouraged us into publication and constantly provided a paradigm of clear reasoning.

Ciaran Driver

1

Investment and Uncertainty: Introduction

1.1 INTRODUCTORY REMARKS

In an influential and pointed attack on Keynes and the post-Keynesians, the late Alan Coddington censured the tradition which locates the source of economic depression in investment under uncertainty. He was particularly concerned to subvert the view that the decentralization of investment decisions leads inevitably to 'chaos and waste' (Coddington 1982, p. 486). For Coddington, neither should private investment be privileged as uniquely affected by uncertainty, nor should uncertainty be regarded as a crippling influence on positive economic plans. Much of this argument is now commonplace; there is no longer much resonance with Keynes' view that 'many of the greatest economic evils of our time are the fruits of risk, uncertainty and ignorance' (1973, vol. IX, p. 291). Rather the benefits of risk taking are now generally accepted.

But have current perceptions exhausted the paths to knowledge? Arguably the present view is a reaction to old-style economic remedies that were clearly not working (Eliasson 1984). The antinomies of market and plan tend to wax and wane with circumstances. This book moves towards an informed judgement on the relative merit of risk as a stimulus, and uncertainty as a dampening force.

The studies in the book constitute some first steps in an evaluation of Coddington's views. We do not – except in conclusion – take issue with his claim that even if uncertainty has negative effects there is little that can be done about it. Rather the book is largely concerned with what seem the more basic questions. Is uncertainty destructive? And if so, is investment the variable that we should be concerned about?

Coddington argues that if uncertainty operates by making economic relationships less determinate, it may do so through its effect on any variable, for example consumer expenditure; Keynes' argument therefore requires an underpinning for the *'relative* unruliness' of investment as a category. This seems the weaker of his two arguments. Consumption expenditure can be contrasted with investment at many levels, as summarized in the following matrix. Investment may here be interpreted broadly to include research and development (R&D) and other long-term commitments.

	consumption	*investment*
avoidable	no	yes
divisible	yes	no
repetitive	yes	no

Each of these characteristics – which are of course stylized – has implications. Firstly, investment is avoidable, i.e. discretionary, which means that it can be independent of current conditions, especially income. This raises the *possibility* that uncertainty will have a disproportionate effect on investment. Secondly, investment is irreversible, occurring in lumpy and context-specific packets; this makes mistakes costly and magnifies the effect of uncertainty, as noted in chapter 4. Thirdly, some – especially large-scale – investment decisions are not repetitive in the sense of being able to learn the underlying stochastic structure governing the outcome. The implication therefore is that decisions have to be made by reference to unknown conditions considerably in the future, when there is little rational basis for knowing how these future conditions are correlated with present ones. As Carvalho (1988) rightly notes, long-term expectations are exogenous because they cannot be definitely related to any current economic variable. The point here, therefore, is that the uncertainty relating to investment decisions is qualitatively different from that arising in respect of regular consumption decisions.

Thus, to summarize the points in reverse order: uncertainty is more severe for investment; the effects of error are more serious for investment decisions; and the opportunities for evading uncertainty by non-action are greater for investment.

It therefore seems that if uncertainty is to have an effect, it will be primarily through investment. Investment is to a certain extent autonomous or independent of other economic variables. This contrasts with orthodox economic theory where investment is generally treated as a passive variable, responding automatically to savings. The discussion in chapter 2 considers the role of investment in orthodox and critical theory.

Investment differs also in another way from consumption: it determines future supply potential. Chapter 3 discusses the specific possibility of capital shortage inhibiting future growth. This issue is addressed because the seriousness (or otherwise) of any negative influence of uncertainty on investment will be amplified in a period where a gap has opened up between potential demand and supply. The discussion here is focused mainly on Europe and is largely empirical. For the reader whose main interest is in the more general results it is possible to pass over this chapter. The remainder of the book is then concerned with risk, uncertainty and their possible influence on investment.

1.2 THE CONSEQUENCE OF UNCERTAINTY FOR INVESTMENT

Coddington (1982) is on firmer ground when he questions whether uncertainty has the sort of effect which it is supposed to have in Keynes' schema. It is worth quoting him on this point:

> If there is great uncertainty surrounding investment decisions and producers respond to this by making, so far as possible, the same investment decisions this period as last period ... this would not result in private sector investments being wayward and unruly; indeed it might result in greater stability than would result from sophisticated calculations based on epistemologically privileged beliefs. (p. 482)

This argument has of course nothing to say about the battery of results that have been developed for investment under calculable risk, discussed in the first sections of chapter 4 of this book. These results show that in many cases a situation of heightened risk would bias investment downward for a profit-maximizing agent even under risk neutrality. But that was not Keynes' concern; his focus and that of the post-Keynesians is on uncertainty proper.

Keynes does not directly dispute Coddington's point. As Lawson (1985) makes clear, Keynes accepted that stability and continuity could result from a conventional response to uncertainty. But Lawson goes on to suggest that uncertainty will produce a temporary stability followed by crisis and structural breaks which portend a period of learning and adaptation (Lawson 1985, pp. 921-2). This mirrors Keynes' own thinking when he remarks that disillusion falls with 'sudden and even catastrophic force ... the expectation is replaced by a contrary error of pessimism' (1973, vol. VII, pp. 316-22).

The question of whether heightened uncertainty would result in greater stability or in a retreat from positive commitments is discussed further in chapter 5 of this book, drawing partly on the work of Ronald Heiner, in particular his seminal paper 'The origin of predictable behaviour' (Heiner 1983). It does not appear possible, however, to resolve this question solely on the plane of theory. The main emphasis in chapter 5 is then on arriving at a measure of uncertainty which can be employed in empirical work to test the effect of uncertainty on investment.

1.3 CONCEPTUALIZING UNCERTAINTY

Empirical estimation requires the construction of measures of uncertainty. Although this is beset with ambiguities, some of these are easy to resolve. For example, there is a common practice of referring to demand uncertainty when what is really intended is demand pessimism, i.e. a general belief that if demand moves anywhere it will be downward.[1] A similar problem of conflating concepts arises in respect of the famous phrase 'animal spirits' which inhabits the works of Keynes, Marx and Freud. Positive animal spirits or 'confidence' are often conflated with a state of mind that is free of uncertainty. But that seems a mistake. Why should a state of high confidence in future prospects not be subject to a band of doubt equal to that of the contrary state? In this book we are concerned with uncertainty rather than confidence; the latter term is generally a conflation of good *and* certain prospects and is rarely used to indicate a sure-bet recession. By contrast the term 'uncertainty', as used in this book, carries no implication for the state of prospect envisaged.

More fundamental ambiguities attend the questions of which variables are experienced as uncertain. Inevitably there is an arbitrary element in the choice of variables, but presumably there is some merit in selecting those variables which have so concerned policy makers that several independent long time series of quarterly forecasts exist. Two such variables are real growth rates and inflation rates.

Having decided the variables in respect of which uncertainty is to be measured, the next step is to suggest a unit of measure. Chapter 5 distinguishes a number of conceptual approaches. These suggest the use of forecast dispersion across forecasting teams reporting in the same quarter as a sensible measure, though it will contain some noise. The dispersion can, depending on the approach, be interpreted as arising from differential ability to deal with environmental complexity or from differential access to information. Whatever its origin it is argued that dispersion will generally be related to average personal uncertainty, since both indicators are driven by the same factors. An alternative approach is to by-pass personal uncertainty altogether and to argue that decision-making difficulty is, at the level of a group, related to the dispersion of opinion within the group which will be proxied by dispersion across forecasting teams.

The dispersion measure of uncertainty contrasts with a more common measure – that of forecast error. On some interpretations, the size of forecast error is a measure of complexity and therefore uncertainty. In chapter 6 it is shown that forecast error helps to determine dispersion but that other factors which might be expected to contribute to uncertainty also have an independent influence on dispersion.

1.4 INVESTMENT EQUATIONS

Uncertainty is rather like fog on the motorway. Drivers might respond to denser fog either by refraining from overtaking as long as the density persists or by a long-lasting decision to reduce speed. The analogy with investment is that uncertainty may engender sustained caution or may simply result in decisions being taken at the last possible moment by post-poning but not cancelling plans. In the latter case, uncertainty may only have a temporary effect. In our empirical work we have looked, when possible, at the permanence or otherwise of any effect of uncertainty on investment. This is given particular attention in chapter 7.

Empirical results are presented in chapters 7 and 8. UK manufacturing plant and machinery investment is the focus of chapter 7, and a number of specifications are reported. Manufacturing was chosen because different approaches to investment are better documented for this sector, as it has been studied far more than say services. The focus is on plant and machinery, partly because the lags are shorter and the equations are easier to specify for the fairly short sample period which is dictated by data availability.[2]

Chapter 8 follows a similar approach but at a disaggregated level. Investment equations here are estimated for different industry groups. For these groups the uncertainty measure used is the dispersion across firms in terms of the entropy implicit in the qualitative response given to survey questions in the form of 'up', 'down' or 'same'. The main survey question used relates to perceptions of optimism by the firm in respect of growth in its industry output.

In some ways the study of investment under uncertainty mirrors the concern – notably in the UK and the US – over the possible effects of 'short-termism', i.e. the tendency to impose short payback criteria on investments in R&D and fixed capital as a result of stock market pressures (Mayer and Alexander 1990). Certainly one of the effects of uncertainty is to shorten payback.[3] Recent literature on investment under uncertainty (e.g. Bernanke 1983) has demonstrated that heightened uncertainty makes waiting for investment more attractive when investments are irreversible. Thus we can infer at least a delay effect of uncertainty on investment, whereby investment funds are either kept liquid, paid out as dividends to keep open the option of equity funding, or invested in projects with 'short-term' payback.

1.5 DOUBTS AND RESERVATIONS: HOPES AND INTENTIONS

Many will doubt the feasibility of the project behind this book. They will argue that uncertainty is inherently unmeasurable or that the expected theoretical response to it by firms is too variable to establish meaningful hypotheses.

Both these criticisms have only limited validity. It is of course true that economic uncertainty will only be part of a broader set of geopolitical and social concerns affecting firms. It is possible also that the same degree of uncertainty will have different effects depending on the extent to which flexibility has evolved to deal with contingent futures. Examples here are the possibilities for hedging, e.g. through leasing or risk sharing with customers, suppliers, financiers or competitors (Ergas 1984).

Nevertheless, if these criticisms dominated, we would not expect to observe significance for the constructed uncertainty variables in investment equations. The criticisms seem to amount to saying either that these variables are noise or that they are entered with misspecification in the equations. These are, of course, testable propositions. Accordingly, for the remainder of the book the doubt 'which often overtakes pioneers ... is put aside as a healthy man puts aside the expectation of death' (Keynes 1973, vol. VII, p. 162).

The importance of the issue can hardly be questioned. Investment behaviour continues to be one of the least well explained of economic aggregates. Uncertainty is a subject for the most part confined to arcane texts, while the associated – often abstruse – models are scarcely ever engaged with empirical data. This book seeks to bring together a consideration of capital investment with a discussion of the nature and measurement of uncertainty. The book breaks fresh ground by establishing measures of uncertainty and studying their effect on investment behaviour.

NOTES

1 For example, Nickell (1978) quotes a National Economic Development Office (NEDO) report suggesting that uncertainty is the single most important discouragement to investment. But the use of the

term 'uncertainty' in that report is so loose that no meaningful conclusions could be drawn.

2 One omission, necessitated by the focus on plant and machinery investment, is any consideration of whether uncertainty alters the balance of investment projects towards the shorter payback end. This is part of a more general omission. The empirical material in chapters 7 and 8 is entirely concerned with the effect of uncertainty on the *quantity* of investment – and only fixed investment at that. It offers no evidence on the nature of investment or its effectiveness. The question of possible 'overinvestment' in the 1960s is discussed briefly in chapter 3, but there is no investigation of the interesting question of the extent to which private investment is socially useless, being merely aimed at appropriation of economic rent.

3 Keynes' well known views on financial speculation were formed in the belief that uncertainty was such that 'investment based on genuine long-term expectation is so difficult today as to be scarcely practicable' (1973, vol. VII, p. 157).

2

Is Investment Important?

2.1 INTRODUCTION

This chapter looks at the importance of capital investment in terms of possible causal links from investment to growth. If investment is an engine of growth, i.e. a causal stimulant, then any depressing influence on investment will result in slower growth with cumulative consequences. Anticipating results from later chapters, we posit a negative effect of uncertainty on both output and capital input. However, the rate of capital formation may have a separate, distinct influence on output growth. It is this latter issue which is the main concern of this chapter. It deals with the transmission to output growth of investment shocks.

Economists have not studied investment with the same intensity as other functional relationships in economics, such as the demand for money. This may reflect two disparate influences. On the one hand, the standard neoclassical growth model accords little or no importance to the autonomous role of investment. On the other hand, the estimation of separate investment functions has proven extremely difficult within the constraints of economic theory. This chapter explores both of these considerations.

Neoclassical, post-Keynesian and 'new' growth theories are examined in sections 2.2 to 2.4 in respect of the role that they accord to investment, and in particular to the causal relationship from investment to growth. Section 2.5 emphasizes the importance of modelling investment and argues that the component of investment due to uncertain expectations needs to be explicitly modelled.

2.2   THE NEOCLASSICAL GROWTH MODEL

In neoclassical growth theory, growth is determined by exogenous technical progress as well as by changes in the labour force, given the parameters of the production function. In this model investment is passive in the sense that investment always takes up available savings. In turn, savings are determined by time preference. Abstracting for the moment from population growth and technical progress, the production function determines the required capital for any output level. Equilibrium output occurs when the savings arising from the output are just compatible with the investment needed to produce that output at the equilibrating rate of interest.

For a given production function with diminishing returns to factors and constant returns to scale, there will be an equilibrium level of output and capital stock. Analysis is often focused on steady state growth, which requires that output and effective inputs grow at the same rate. With no technical progress, exogenous population growth is the only influence on the steady state growth. Of course the propensity to save can increase, but this is expected merely to lead to increased capital deepening via interest rate movements as the economy adjusts towards a new steady state.[1]

Analysing steady state with full employment has limited relevance. But even abstracting from steady state assumptions, neoclassical theory accords a very modest role to capital formation, because the presumption is that getting entrepreneurs to invest presents no problem.

This is best demonstrated in the context of a production function with constant returns to scale. It is convenient to represent it in growth terms as

$$x = g + \beta k + \alpha l \tag{2.1}$$

where x, k and l are the rates of growth of output, capital and labour and where β and α are the elasticities of capital and labour with respect to output, summing to one for the constant returns assumption. Writing y for $x - l$, the growth of output per person, we get

$$y = g + \beta(k - l) \qquad (2.2)$$

This framework can be used to ask about the effect of changes in the capital–labour ratio.

From (2.2) is easy to see that the contribution of capital–labour ratio growth $(k - l)$ to growth of labour productivity y is given by the product of β and the particular value of $k - l$ that occurs in any period. Nordhaus (1982, p. 143) estimated β by the share of profits in income for a number of OECD countries, and reckoned that change in capital–labour growth could only account for a small part of the slowdown in labour productivity in the 1970s.[2]

This approach can be criticized on a number of grounds. Firstly, if technology is largely embodied in capital goods, it is to be expected that new vintages of capital have higher productivities. Secondly, in so far as capital growth may determine output growth (see Figure 2.2) there is a further interaction effect on productivity which operates when economies of scale exist.[3] So, while it may be true that the general slowdown in productivity in the 1970s was not investment led, the interpretation of the role of capital formation is more complex than is often assumed.

2.3 THE CONTRIBUTIONS OF KALDOR AND ARROW

Nevertheless, even some of the sternest critics of the neoclassical framework, such as Kaldor, did not disagree that the role of capital accumulation was confined to short-term variations in the growth rate. This can most simply be seen in a non-vintage context by generalizing the derivation of (2.2) to the case where there are static economies of scale, i.e. $\alpha + \beta \neq 1$. Letting $\alpha + \beta = p$, we get

$$y = g + \beta(k - l) + (p - 1)l$$
$$y = g + \beta(k - l) + (p - 1)(x - y)$$

$$y = \frac{g}{p} + \frac{\beta}{p}(k - l) + \left(\frac{p-1}{p}\right)x \qquad (2.3)$$

Thus, increasing static returns carry over into dynamic relationships; output growth will have an influence on labour productivity growth, in addition to a contribution from growth of the capital-labour ratio. This derivation from a traditional production function with increasing returns is simply a convenient way of arriving at a linear version of Kaldor's augmented technical progress function, where the last term is usually referred to as the Verdoorn effect and the β/p coefficient captures the relationship between labour productivity and capital deepening due to embodiment of technology and learning (Michl 1985). This can be sketched as

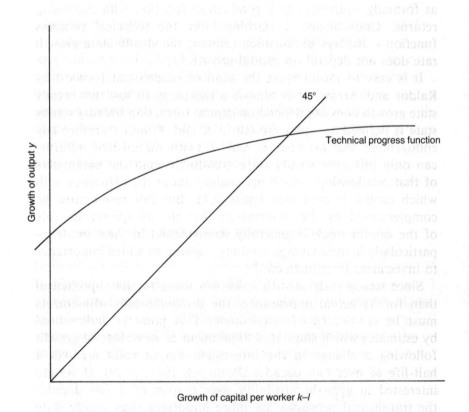

FIGURE 2.1   Steady state growth is independent of investment

in figure 2.1, from which it can be seen that the steady state growth of output, if it exists, is independent of investment but depends on the influences on the height of the technical progress function above the origin – in the main, higher-quality business management and scientific education (Kaldor and Mirrlees 1962).[4]

Only if there is a continuous improvement in such quality factors will the permanent growth rate be sustained at a higher level. This is also the conclusion of the formal models of 'learning by doing' (Arrow 1962). In these models the rate of technical progress is determined by cumulative past output of the capital goods on the assumption that learning takes place primarily in the construction of machines. Arrow makes labour efficiency depend on the capital stock; this increases the capital coefficient in the production function so that learning can be interpreted as formally equivalent to a production function with increasing returns. Once again, if learning – like the technical progress function – displays diminishing returns, the steady state growth rate does not depend on capital growth.[5]

It is easy to misinterpret the kind of models put forward by Kaldor and Arrow. It is almost a tautology to say that steady state growth does not depend on capital formation because steady state is defined as equal growth in K and Y, and therefore any endogenous link between K and Y (with diminishing returns) can only influence steady state growth through the parameters of that relationship, which are mainly about the efficiency with which capital is used (see figure 2.1). But this result must be complemented by the observation that the disequilibrium role of the capital stock is generally strengthened in these models – particularly in their vintage versions – giving an added importance to investment in adjustment.[6]

Since steady state growth is known more for its hypothetical than for its actual appearance, the disequilibrium adjustments must be considered of importance. This point is underscored by estimates which show that adjustment to new rates of growth following a change in the investment–output ratio involves a half-life of over two decades (Bombach 1985, p. 29). If we are interested in growth possibility over a span of a few decades the transitional processes are more important than steady state theorizing. As Matthews et al. (1982) note: 'If [capital] elasticities are high, changes in the investment income ratio may have a major effect on the growth rate and may be more important than any exogenous changes in the rate of technical progress' (p. 327).

2.4 NEW GROWTH THEORY

An alternative account of the importance of investment for growth goes by the name 'new growth theory' (Romer 1986; Baldwin 1989). This suggests the existence of increasing returns largely external to the firm due, say, to technological spillover benefits to other firms. If capital–output elasticity is really – as generally assumed – about 0.3, then the bulk of change in output per worker will inevitably be explained by the residual g in (2.2), usually termed 'technical progress' or 'total factor productivity'. This is because there is a long-term tendency for the growth of output per worker to move in line with growth in capital per worker. The new growth theory simply reinterprets the historical evidence and estimates β equal to unity, leaving no residual disembodied technical progress. The implication of the new growth theory is an increased importance for fixed investment, though, as Baldwin (1989) notes, 'the jury is still out on the importance of scale economies at economy-wide level' (p. 257).[7]

The distinct quality of this theory does not lie in any qualitatively different conclusion about steady state growth if $\beta < 1$. But the closer β is to one, the more sustained will be the improvement in growth possible arising from any exogenous one-off improvement in the output–capital ratio, assuming that the savings (= investment) rate does not compensate in the opposite direction. The most powerful conclusion of the model is that, when $\beta = 1$, the long-term growth rate depends on the savings ratio since each unit of capital generates output with an elasticity of unity.[8] This replicates the traditional knife-edge problem of Harrod (Sen 1970), where a constant capital–output ratio also makes growth depend on the savings rate.

Some commentators have pointed to the implausibility of the capital coefficient being exactly one; it cannot be greater if growth is not to be explosive. However, the coefficient may be unity for certain periods, in which case lack of diminishing returns to capital closes off both the neoclassical and the Kaldor-Arrow determination of steady state growth, focusing attention on the proportion of income saved or invested.[9]

It must be said that there is nothing especially 'new' about this conclusion that the savings ratio affects growth; it is sometimes known as a classical – as opposed to a neoclassical – view. It is also defended strongly by some economists, notably Eltis (1966). The argument here is that technology is embodied in new capital vintages and that the greater the proportion of income saved and invested, the more technological progress will be generated. In contrast to Kaldor's technical progress function where growth depends on the capital growth rate, here it depends

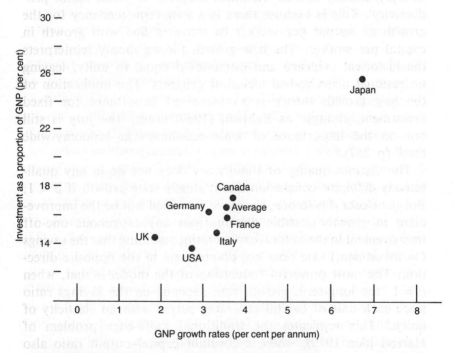

FIGURE 2.2 Growth rates and ratios of gross non-residential investment to GNP in the major OECD economies, 1960–1985

Source: Bank of England *Quarterly Bulletin*, June 1986

on the share of investment. Eltis argues that the logic of Kaldor's position implies his version of the technical progress function.

Some evidence for the Eltis position is contained in figure 2.2. Although the data are only suggestive and would require extensive modelling for formal testing to be possible, the pattern does not seem supportive of the neoclassical position that the share of investment is irrelevant to growth over the long term.

2.5 AN AUTONOMOUS INVESTMENT FUNCTION

At the outset of this chapter we raised the question of why investment behaviour was a Cinderella study in economics. The first answer was the view held by some that investment 'does not matter'. It can now be seen that there is more than one version of this view. Either the savings and investment ratio is irrelevant to growth (neoclassical view), or the savings rate does matter but it determines the investment rate. The latter is implicitly the Eltis position, as there is no independent investment function in his work. Put differently, it is the savings decision – òr its counterpart, the consumption function – that is of chief interest.

But for many, especially in the post-Keynesian tradition, investment does matter; so why has it not been more closely studied? Perhaps the reason is that investment is seen as partly autonomous, depending on exogenous variables such as the state of confidence which cannot easily be quantified without falling into tautology.

The theory necessary to explain variation in investment is often seen as fuzzy, encompassing 'historical, political and psychological characteristics of an economy' (Robinson 1962, p. 37; quoted in Hacche 1979, p. 170). The models that best explain investment are accelerator models (Clark 1979; Catinat et al. 1987; Hunter and Pescetto 1991), but Matthews et al. (1982) remind us of their inadequacy: 'These [output] effects can scarcely account for the *continuous* falling off in the rate of capital formation that occurred after the beginning of the 1960s' (p. 389).[10] These authors invoke the notion of 'waning of confidence' that occurred during the 1960s.[11] This is echoed in a major Organization for Economic Cooperation and Development (OECD) report

(McCracken et al. 1977), which referred to a 'significant reversal in entrepreneurs' attitudes towards risk' (p. 163).

We have thus come full circle. Even those who argue that investment is important for growth *and* is autonomous have failed to address it adequately, precisely because of the difficulty of quantifying the autonomous influences. The role of this chapter has been to establish the possible importance of investment for growth and hence to establish the importance of being able to quantify the hitherto elusive notion of the degree of certainty or confidence in future estimations of profitable demand.

The latter issue is addressed in chapter 5 onwards. Here it may be noted that the effect of investment for growth may matter more in certain periods than others. In particular, competitive advantage gained early in the life cycle of an industry may persist for many years (Porter 1989). The experience of the US semiconductor industry from the early 1960s is a case in point; heavy investment to meet government-induced demand assured a commanding lead, especially over European suppliers (Malerba 1985). Such opportunities for growth in new product markets will be most pronounced in periods of structural change, as labour processes, technology and patterns of consumer demand show unusual variation. But it is precisely in such periods that economic uncertainty is at its height. Thus, uncertainty may be doubly important for growth in that it may most seriously limit investment precisely when investment is most important for future growth prospects, i.e. at times of unusual structural change. Evidence is presented in the next chapter that heightened structural change has occurred and that the result may be a legacy of 'capital shortage'.

2.6 CONCLUSIONS

This chapter has surveyed several approaches to the theory of long-run growth. In so doing it has questioned the argument that investment ratios do not influence growth. The discussion has shown the need for better understanding of the investment decision, and in particular the need to relate actual investment behaviour to states of uncertainty. The latter is the focus of the book as a whole. It has also been argued that investment is especially important for growth during periods of unusual structural change. However, structural change spawns uncertainty (Eliasson and Fries 1983), so it is precisely in such periods that investment will be inhibited, leading to a possible capital shortage. The next chapter will discuss the evidence for this capital shortage position for the current period.

NOTES

1 The Harrod model yields exactly opposite conclusions to the neoclassical model in regard to the stability of growth by failing to assume that investment mirrors savings.

2 This is regarded among many US economists as incontrovertible, since the growth of the capital–labour ratio increased after the first oil shock as productivity fell.

3 A possible theoretical underpinning for this is the model of Romer (1986).

4 In the context of the model just described, one-off increases in capital productivity such as reductions in defence expenditure or trade liberalization would have effects that were purely temporary, as in the neoclassical model.

5 Since learning increases the capital coefficient β, the learning parameters can be seen to affect the slope of the technical progress function and thus the steady state growth rate.

6 The models of Kaldor and Arrow are attempts to show how steady state might be implied by models other than neoclassical ones. But in doing so they bring out some of the problems with the latter. For example, learning implies that capital is not paid its marginal product, so on this ground alone there must be a problem with equating (via the interest rate) savings in the neoclassical model with steady state investment growth. If independent investment functions are introduced, as in Kaldor's models, they will lead to equilibrium growth only under fairly restrictive assumptions (Hacche 1979). In particular, an independent investment function can lead to explosive growth or stagnation depending on how it interacts with the savings function. These models therefore raise the possibility that capital formation can fall short of requirements.

7 It may be noted that a β of unity interpreted differently in the Arrow framework of 'learning by doing' would imply an elasticity

of unity for labour efficiency with respect to cumulative investment.

8 This reinstates that Cambridge growth equation, where growth is the savings rate over the capital–output ratio.

9 Romer (1990) cautions against a simple policy response of subsidy to physical capital, since the output of research activity may not, as in his 1986 model, be coupled with increases in physical capital.

10 This conclusion was reached using the capital stock estimates, since revised downwards, which will moderate the downward movement in the rate of growth of capital.

11 Another example of this is manufacturing in Britain in the interwar period 1929–37, which was characterized by an output recovery far stronger than the British boom of the 1980s (Rowthorn 1989). Capital formation, however, grew remarkably slowly and the capital–labour ratio actually fell. Confidence had been affected by the preceding slump, and industry was taken by surprise at the strength of output. Internal finance would have been too restricted to allow for a rapid expansion in investment, and manufacturers preferred to raise utilization levels. 'Not only had industry failed to invest enough to provide in advance for the increase in output but when the increase in output came there were fears that it would be transitory' (Matthews et al. 1982, p. 384).

3

Capital Shortage and Trends in Investment

3.1 INTRODUCTION

This chapter is concerned with the question of whether there is an impending 'capital shortage' in Europe, and particularly in the UK. The issue is of intrinsic interest, but it is also important in the context of this book in that economic uncertainty may lead to capital shortage by depressing investment. Furthermore, as noted in the previous chapter, capital shortage can be expected to have greatest adverse implications for growth in periods of heightened structural change when opportunities for market expansions are enhanced. Since such periods of unusual structural change also engender uncertainty, the conditions of capital shortage are most likely when they are most damaging. Section 3.2 discusses the definition of capital shortage. The roles of the capital–output ratio and of accelerated scrapping in explaining capital shortage are discussed in sections 3.3 and 3.4. Section 3.5 suggests that capital shortage can arise as a result of uncertainty induced by rapid structural change.

3.2 CAPITAL SHORTAGE

Capital shortage was raised as a possibility in the wake of the first oil shock; it formed an important part of the McCracken et al. (1977) report, and also featured in works by Malinvaud (1977; 1982). The argument is that slow growth and unemployment will remain a long-term problem because of capacity shortages even if any real wage gaps are eliminated. Subsequently the view was echoed by researchers at the London Business School in the mid 1980s; it was argued that the UK economy then was close to capacity and that capital constraints in manufacturing would hamper expansion (Robinson and Wade 1985). More recently the argument has surfaced again in relation to European economies (Bean 1989).

One initial complication is that the term 'capital shortage' is used in different ways – as is the associated term 'investment requirements'. It is fairly obvious that whether a capital shortage exists depends on what target growth rate is considered reasonable and what economic considerations (relative prices, utilization of factors, technology etc.) are to be taken as given in calculating an implied path for required invesment.

Is it possible to define a required rate of investment? In the neoclassical model the capital–output ratio is endogenous and perfectly flexible in response to savings, so that there is no such thing as a required rate of growth of capital independent of choices on savings. Most practical-minded economists and organizations see things differently. For example, the McCracken et al. (1977) OECD report defined a 'required rate of investment' as that needed to generate sufficient capacity to meet a given target output growth, where the margin of price flexibility was assumed to be fairly small (p. 295).

One way of approaching the problem is to work with a model which identifies which barrier to growth is likely to be binding. For example, if the operation of the labour market is likely to constrain growth to low levels, it is sometimes argued that capital shortage is unlikely to impose a serious constraint. Schultze (1987) worked out investment requirements in this way corresponding to growth warranted by non-inflationary conditions. His calculations implied rather moderate investment requirements for most European countries – though the target growth was equally modest, being aimed at simply absorbing increases in labour supply up to 1990. The problem with this kind of approach is (we suspect) that it is very sensitive to the linkages between the various parts of the overall model. For example, if there is no feedback in the model from new capital vintage to the labour market, the conditions for non-inflationary growth are likely to be misrepresented. But it is certain that a period of investment – aimed, say, at replacing scrapped equipment – will raise labour productivity for a time and permit higher real wages without necessarily adding to inflationary pressure.

Since the links from capital investment to productivity and thus to warranted wages and inflationary pressure are difficult to gauge at all accurately, investment requirements will not be assessed here in this way. An alternative approach is to assume that price flexibility and substitutability are limited so that capital growth can determine output growth.

Denoting output by Y, net capital stock by K, gross investment by GI and depreciation by D, and using a dot for growth rates, we have

$$\dot{K} = \frac{GI - D}{Y} \; \frac{Y}{K} \qquad (3.1)$$

If the target rate of growth is unchanged, so too is $\dot{K}$. The gross investment requirement GI should also be unchanged unless one of two conditions changes. Firstly, a rise in the capital–output ratio for independent reasons could increase the required investment to sustain a given target of capacity growth. Secondly, accelerated scrapping (a rise in D) may necessitate a fairly sustained rise in the ratio of gross investment to income. We deal with the two questions of capital–output ratio and accelerated scrapping in sections 3.3 and 3.4.

3.3 THE CAPITAL–OUTPUT RATIO

The long-standing concern in the literature about a possible capital shortage stemmed from a conjunction of lower rates of capital formation and a rising capital–output ratio – at least until the early 1980s. Trends in capital formation and in capital–labour substitution are shown in table 3.1.

From the late 1960s to the early 1980s there was a trend upwards in the capital–output ratio in most European countries. This is a real effect, for although the rise is attributable partly to the valuation effect of higher prices for capital goods and partly to lower utilization of capital, these qualifications are of minor

TABLE 3.1 European Community investment and capital intensity (per cent per year)

	1973/1960	1981/1973	1986/1981	1990/1986
Real gross fixed capital formation	5.6	−0.3	1.1	6.1
Real investment in equipment	5.4	1.2	2.9	8.4
Capital intensity	4.9	3.6	2.3	1.4
Capital–output ratio	0.4	1.5	0.3	−0.4

Source: European Commission

importance (Schultze 1987).[1]

Although most discussions of capital shortage are premised on the argument of excessive capital–output ratios (Bean 1989), we have relegated the arguments to appendix 3.1. The reason for this is partly that the undoubted rise in capital–labour ratios that characterized the 1960s to the 1980s is only tangentially related to the interplay of capital shortage with uncertainty. But more importantly, table 3.1 shows that there has recently been a reversal in the trend of the capital–output ratio.[2]

The improvement in capital productivity in the 1980s was especially marked for UK manufacturing; a 10 per cent output growth occurred with very little net investment.[3] The question arises as to how sustainable these developments are, i.e. whether they will translate into a long-term reduction in investment requirements.

The sustainability of the improvement in capital productivity is problematic. Environmental and energy-saving measures will continue to require extra capital for no extra (recorded) output.[4] And there must be some doubts over the permanence of recent improvements in the utilization of assets, e.g. through increased shift work or greater managerial efficacy. Nevertheless there must be a supposition from the nature of recent technological progress that greater utilization of all factors of production will be ongoing. Data on the diffusion of new technology suggest that there is still potential for such technological improvement (Northcott and Walling 1988).

It appears then that any argument in support of future capital shortage cannot be based on the prospect of a rise in the long-run capital–output ratio. If anything, the reverse is likely to be true.

3.4   ACCELERATED SCRAPPING

The second reason why gross investment requirements may have risen concerns the accelerated scrapping of capital stock. This means retirement for economic reasons beyond the level of retirement anticipated solely on the basis of assets coming to the end of their physical life. Appendix 3.2 discusses the evidence that accelerated scrapping took place in response to the two oil shocks and recent recessions. The general consensus is that such scrapping has been substantial.

The effects on required investment are of course only transitory, but they may be significantly large and will use up investible funds. Even on the basis of official capital stock figures, net investment in UK manufacturing in the first half of the 1980s was negative by about 3.5 per cent, i.e. gross investment did not cover depreciation. With accelerated scrapping of 5 per cent or so during this period, a considerable shortfall from previous levels is indicated. But subsequent investment has been only moderate, even in growth years.

Accelerated scrapping implies the need for greater investment to compensate for higher depreciation. But a need to compensate for greater depreciation may occur even with normal scrapping if the age of the capital stock is rising. In such a case, normal depreciation may rise for a period of years, requiring higher gross investment if the net capital stock is not to shrink.

The figures for UK manufacturing, shown in table 3.2, suggest that for much of the 1970s and 1980s normal depreciation – quite apart from accelerated scrapping – was causing the net capital stock to grow much slower than gross investment.

Once allowance is made for accelerated scrapping, it may be surmised that a good deal of investible funds is needed just to provide sufficient capital to maintain previous growth trends.[5] The gravity of this is reinforced by the considerable fall-off in

TABLE 3.2 UK manufacturing ratio of investment to GDP (including leasing)

	Gross	Net
1973–79	11.5	3.1
1979–82	10.5	0.7
1982–85	10.3	0.1
1986–89	11.0	2.0

Sources: National Economic Development Office; Central Statistical Office

investment in the early 1990s in response to global recession and heightened uncertainty.

In some ways it is misleading to focus on the ratio of investment to output because they are, of course, interdependent. If attention is given to the simple rate of growth of the capital stock or of capital-labour ratios, there has been quite a marked decline in the last two decades; for example, a fall from a peak growth of about 4 per cent a year in the gross capital stock at the end of the 1960s in the UK to less than half that in recent years, and much lower still in manufacturing.

3.5 STRUCTURAL CHANGE AND UNCERTAINTY

Quite apart from any shortfall in capital due to previous investment behaviour, there is an argument that investment is limited, now and in the future, by the uncertainty that attends the structural change which the economy is experiencing. Arguably, structural change, by lessening incremental rather than radical adjustments, increases the uncertainty or ignorance over the future evolution of the economy and might weaken the response of investment to improved profitability. Certainly – at least in the UK – structural change has accelerated in recent years (Driver 1990; Driver and Dunne 1991).

The pace of this structural change creates both opportunities and problems. It is not just that markets for new products are opened up by faster technological growth; the supply potential of the economy is also strengthened. Freeman and Soete (1987) refer to the 'dramatic potential offered through IT [information technology] to separate actual production from control, administration, design, management and marketing' and 'savings in all factors of production' (pp. 251–4).

Many of these developments, however, imply non-incremental structural change. New patterns of output and expenditure tend to be bound up with new social conditions such as patterns of work, distributional changes, legal arrangements, reorientation of trade and changes in the conditions of trade, variable acceptance of new technology, changes in the education system and so on (Driver 1987, pp. 78–87). The pervasiveness of these changes makes forecasting more than usually difficult. Accordingly, there may be a positive relationship between structural change and uncertainty. Consistent data to test this hypothesis over a long period are not available. However, comparable annual data can be used for the short range 1977 to 1985, for which period a value of 0.56 is obtained for the simple correlation coefficient between the variables.[6] This relationship between structural change and uncertainty raises the possibility that although profitability may be enhanced by structural change, the response to this in the form of long-term commitments such as investment may be weakened.[7] Some indirect evidence for the view that the investment response has weakened is given in table 3.3. In addition, a frequency analysis of replies (Junankar 1989) reveals a slight fall in payback period from five years earlier. The evidence of these studies, where available, suggests that real required rates of return have also increased over the years.

There is some evidence then that the investment response to increased profitability has weakened. Much of the restoration of profitability in Europe has been due to wage moderation, and thus there is an ambiguous effect of demand (Malinvaud

TABLE 3.3   Required payback periods of UK firms

Source	Payback (years)
Rockley 1973	2–5
NEDO 1982	2–4
NEDO 1986	1–4

1982; Klau 1984). Furthermore, in so far as profitability has been restored in some sectors by a rise in capital productivity, the resultant problems of structural change also raise questions about future patterns of growth. Put simply, uncertainty may tend to qualify the role of profitability in raising the animal spirits of business investors. This hypothesis is the focus of the empirical work in chapter 7.

3.6   CONCLUSIONS

The notion that capital shortage is a constraint on growth and employment is one that has been heard in Europe for nearly two decades. In most versions of the argument it is simply a way of saying that real wages have been too high in the past, depressing investment and making whatever investment there was more capital intensive. Given that capital is generally not reversible, slower growth of real wages will only provide solutions in the very long run. According to this story, the rise in the capital–output ratio experienced in most European economies in the period up to the early 1980s was a result of diminishing returns to capital as its intensity increased in response to relative factor costs.

We have argued for a different version, whereby capital shortage reflects a faster pace of depreciation on the one hand and slower capital accumulation in response to uncertain demand on the other. New technology offers opportunities for rapid growth, but economic uncertainty – itself the result of the turbulence of economic change – tends to inhibit capital formation and stifle growth. This version of the capital shortage thesis implies that investment is constrained by uncertainty, a proposition that is investigated in chapters 7 and 8. The next three chapters are given over to a consideration of the nature and role of uncertainty in investment models.

APPENDIX 3.1:   EXPLANATIONS FOR CAPITAL SHORTAGE

Perhaps surprisingly, a standard explanation of capital shortage is wage push, resulting in high capital intensity and leading to a fall in capital productivity at the margin. In turn this results in a growth of output and capital insufficient to absorb the labour released in the earlier process of capital intensification. Unemployment rises in consequence. The situation is not strictly one of capital shortage since investment is at the margin encountering diminishing returns. But growth is not sufficient to absorb the labour force. Thus there is a policy dilemma.

Although this explanation is not necessarily the most plausible one, the arguments are set out in the following section because this explanation has dominated thinking about capital shortage in recent years. The subsequent section develops an alternative explanation for the evolution of the capital–labour and capital–output ratios.

The role of real wages

It is quite natural for real wages to rise and for the capital–output ratio to remain fairly constant. This was the historical pattern for most of the century of UK economic growth surveyed by Matthews et al. (1982). What appeared to happen was that the capital–labour substitution that occurred along with a rise in real wages was just compensated by technological progress, which offset the diminishing returns from greater capital intensity. The endogenous forces that kept this balance could have been upset by any external influence, e.g. external competition, autonomous trade union militancy or a fall-off in technological opportunity.

The most common explanation for the rise in the capital–output ratio from the late 1960s was that real wages were rising faster than technological change was able to compensate for, thus reducing the marginal productivity of capital as capital deepening occurred. The fall in marginal productivity was partly due to the limits of increasing returns to scale and the incremental nature of investment (Freeman 1985). Arguments in this vein are put forward by McCracken et al. (1977), Matthews et al. (1982) and Bean (1989). A rider is sometimes added to the effect that increased capital incentives accentuated the process, and some view the slowdown in growth as the prime impulse that drove up relative real wages.

At first sight of the empirical evidence, the general argument does not even seem plausible. Although a continued rise in the capital–labour ratio K/L in the face of a falling output–capital ratio Y/K is consistent with an argument that relative prices were exerting an independent influence, such an explanation has limited hold on reality for the 1970s and 1980s. As shown in figure 3.1, for the UK, capital–labour substitution seemed to continue despite a stabilization of relative price movements.

The argument may be made consistent with the facts by adopting a disequilibrium approach whereby the relevant stimulus to invest-

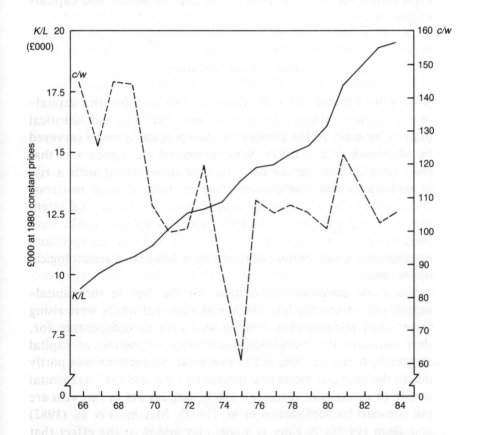

FIGURE 3.1 Net capital stock per employee in manufacturing K/L (£000 at 1980 constant prices) and relative factor prices c/w (real costs capital/labour)

ment is profitability rather than the cost of capital. Schultze (1987) argues that European countries in the first couple of decades after the war were able to incorporate new technology from the frontier country – the US. Since there was a scarcity of capital, rates of return were driven up to abnormal levels and 'the heavy investment in capital–labour substitution that was made in response to these initially high rates of return gradually drove down the output–capital ratio and reduced rates of return ... And, of course, as rates of return fell so did the volume of investment' (p. 524). This is a rather curious story of the boom and bust variety; the reader may find the actual explanation of the process by which capital–labour substitution went 'too far' somewhat elusive.[8] Nevertheless, the emphasis in Schultze (1987) on profitability reinforces the point made earlier by Malinvaud (1982) that the investment decision must be modelled as a response to disequilibrium.

The relative price argument – or too high real wages in the past – can therefore lead directly to a 'capital shortage' problem that can only slowly be resolved. Bean (1989) estimates that steps to roughly halve European unemployment in a few years would require either a sustained 20 per cent increase in investment or a permanent 50 per cent fall in relative labour costs to encourage substitution.

Alternative to the relative price argument

An alternative explanation can be offered for the rising capital–labour and capital–output ratios of the 1970s. This approach suggests that the main reasons for capital–labour substitution were shifts in technology and a drive for higher quality which necessitated re-equipment. This view is supported by economists close to industry sectors (NEDC 1987). It is consistent with this approach to see real wages as *responding* to the substitution of capital for labour rather than initiating that process. Outdated labour practices associated with previous modes of production and vintages of equipment were bought out by management, so raising the real wages of those retained in employment. Of course the incidence of this will be highest among the most advanced firms in any sector, and the remainder will experience wages driven up by competition along the lines discussed earlier.

Until the late 1960s the capital–output ratio was fairly stable, implying that capital–labour substitution was compatible with the stable wage share that prevailed. What needs to be explained is the continued capital intensification despite a fall-off in capital productivity beyond that date. How does the second account square this decline in productivity with a freely chosen continuation of capital–labour substitution?

There is no puzzle about capital intensive industries. Employment in those sectors declined faster than the capital stock since scrapping was delayed. In other industries, where growth opportunities existed, there were possibilities of expansion with new investment. In theory this should have led to a lower capital–output ratio due to the application of new technology. In particular, information technology seems to open up the possibility of productivity growth in relation to all factor inputs (Freeman and Soete 1987, p. 238; Soete 1985, p. 73).

But it seems that in the expanding industries of the 1970s the marginal product of capital, defined as best practice capital productivity, was low – not because of diminishing returns but owing to a perverse reaction to the novelty of technical change (see Gold 1979, p. 75; Freeman and Soete 1987, p. 68). Often investment initially increases the capital–output ratio, for a number of disequilibrium reasons. Firstly, the increase in investment is often disproportionately higher in the short run than the increase in productive capacity, given the ability of depreciated machinery to deliver production unrelated to its value. Secondly, new technology commands a premium price at least until multiple sourcing is the norm. And thirdly, there is often an extended period of learning on new equipment and associated externalities such as lack of skills or network externalities. However, the long-term advantages of the new technology dictate – independently of relative prices – the move towards greater capital intensity.

It may be that with faster capital growth these problems are lessened. If so it would be one explanation of why the United States seemed to experience a slower rise in capital–output ratio than Europe from the late 1960s to the early 1980s (Schultze 1987). Certainly there is evidence from the United States that later vintages of capital were resulting in an acceleration of embodied technical progress, offsetting other influences on labour productivity (McHugh and Lane 1987).

The technological explanation for the movements in capital intensity and the capital–output ratio is complementary rather than opposed to the explanation based on relative prices. Nevertheless there are important differences between the conclusions that may be drawn. In the technological approach, the recent stabilization of the capital–output ratio already reflects heightened opportunities for long-run profitability due to technical change.

APPENDIX 3.2:   ACCELERATED SCRAPPING IN UK
MANUFACTURING

Accelerated scrapping can imply capital shortage if gross investment does not rise to compensate. The discussion here is again confined to the UK since there is a need to rely on sources other than official statistics. One method of estimating the degree of scrapping is to treat the disposals data in the census of production as proxies for scrapping. This formed the basis of a model of scrapping in Driver (1986). The real value of disposals in manufacturing rose sharply over the 1980s.

The disposals data are pro-cyclical, and their use as a proxy for scrapping has been criticized by Bosworth (1988), who argues that the data represent *sales* of second-hand equipment and can therefore deviate from scrapping activity. However, Bosworth's own study of machine counts in three industries (textiles, machine tools, and iron and steel) also lead him to argue that idle capital has generally been scrapped and that the official measures of the capital stock tend to overstate the true capacity of the economy.

An indirect method of estimating scrapping has been given in Mendis and Muellbauer (1984), using split time trends in a production function and attributing the productivity slowdown 1973–80 to cumulative measurement error in the capital stock. Assuming (implausibly?) that this was the only factor behind the slowdown, the official figures would overstate the manufacturing capital stock by 35 per cent in 1980.

It is interesting to note that this figure is identical to that obtained by a quite different method by Smith (1987) for the year 1983. He looked at a sample of companies reporting on the inflation-adjusted or current cost account (CCA) method of accounting. He extracted data on equipment only – as property values are not treated in company accounts in the same way as in the national accounts. His finding was that the official gross capital stock was overestimated by 35 per cent for manufacturing and that asset lives should be 16 years rather than 26. Estimates were also given of the capital stock by industry group and also for non-manufacturing. These results are interesting and plausible, and suffer only from some doubtful assumptions such as equal capital–labour ratios for domestic and overseas assets – an assumption needed to allocate the capital stock in the accounts to areas of operation.

A much quoted work that attempted a direct estimate of scrapping is Wadhwani and Wall (1986). Their estimates are also based on company accounts data for a sample of companies whose accounts were based on replacement value for 1980–3. Unlike Smith, however, they include property in their comparisons with the official figures and their figures are for the net stock. The inclusion of property may account for the rather peculiar pattern of discrepancies that they obtained, with the official figures suggested as *underestimating* the stock in 1980–1 and *overestimating* it by about 2 per cent in 1983. These figures have to be interpreted with great caution, not only because of the inclusion of inappropriate property comparisons, but also because the company data used by these authors exclude bankruptcies; are biased towards large companies; may have selection bias due to the voluntary nature of the accounting system; and include overseas activities of the firms. In a second part to their study the authors try to adjust the historical price estimates of capital stock to form a longer time series based on the company accounts. Unfortunately the estimates of the extent of scrapping are very sensitive to the assumed age of the scrapped assets (Driver 1989, p. 29), ranging from 2 to 16 per cent of the capital stock. Their preferred estimate of scrapping gives implausible lifespans for scrapped equipment.

Finally, a further possible proxy for scrapping has been proposed in Driver (1989). This is the index of demolitions of industrial floorspace for England and Wales produced by the

Department of the Environment. These data show a sharp increase after 1981 which was sustained at least until the mid 1980s, when the statistical series was discontinued. Driver's estimates, based on this and other sources, suggest an extra 1 per cent loss of the manufacturing capital stock for each year of accelerated scrapping in the 1980s.

NOTES

1 Also apparently of minor importance were composition changes in output and increased environmental and energy capital expenditures (Matthews et al. 1982, p. 338).

2 Part of the reason for this is the higher utilization levels now typical in most industries, but the change in the ratio seems more than cyclical. Over time the capital–output ratio ceased to rise as old plant was scrapped and the beneficial effects of new technology began to flow more freely.

3 The capital stock data do not account for extra quality of machinery if the quality improvements are costless. Since this is likely as microelectronics are introduced, the 'real' expenditure on capital stock is arguably not an accurate indicator of the 'volume'.

4 Some estimates put the increased requirements in the region of 2 per cent of GDP. See the discussion of estimates by Phillips and Drew in the *Financial Times*, 31 May 1990.

5 For the business sector as a whole, OECD sources show a similar pattern for all main countries. Net ratios of investment to output were lower from 1976 to 1986, before recovering, especially in Europe (*Economic Outlook*, December 1989). The OECD has also drawn attention to the fact that both savings and investment rates in most countries are lower now than in the 1960s (*Economic Studies*, June 1990). We have not addressed the question of savings rates as a constraint on investment in this chapter, where the emphasis is on autonomous investment behaviour.

6 The Nickell index of structural change (Newell 1984) was used as updated in Driver (1991), as this provides the longest timespan with consistent data. This was correlated with growth uncertainty, as defined in chapter 6.

7 This is most likely to be true of expansionary investment, which involves commitments to future potential markets. On the other hand, capital deepening to gain efficiency is a form of investment

that minimizes uncertainty both because the paybacks are generally shorter and because only local knowledge is needed to judge the effect of this investment on costs. By contrast, expansionary investment needs knowledge of contingencies that shape market demand.

8 Kindleberger (1967) points to the role of labour reserves in Europe as an influence holding down real wages post-war. He predicted that the virtuous cycle would eventually be broken by labour shortages.

4

Investment under Risk

This chapter looks at possible mechanisms or channels by which uncertainty may affect investment. We do not distinguish here between risk and uncertainty, leaving that to the next chapter. In section 4.2 we distinguish between financial risk and total project risk. Section 4.3 investigates the role of non-linearities such as risk aversion in causing a decision variable to vary with uncertainty. Section 4.4 extends this discussion to include disequilibrium. The particular features of capital input decisions are outlined in section 4.5. A discussion of the role of uncertainty under oligopoly is contained in section 4.6. Section 4.7 is concerned with possible methodological shortcomings of the theoretical models, arguing that they do not fully represent the actual responses that firms make to uncertainty.

Since this chapter is the least reader-friendly in the book – at least for those who do not enjoy working through third partial derivatives – it is arranged so that the general message can be gleaned from a reading of the text alone.

4.2 TYPES OF INVESTMENT RISK

There are a number of distinct conceptual approaches to understanding the role of risk in investment appraisal. Most importantly, we need to be clear whether we are adopting

• a manager oriented *or* a shareholder oriented analysis;

• a project based *or* a firm based analysis.

In modern financial theory, risk is important for the shareholder only in so far as it is not diversifiable. Holding a balanced, diversified portfolio of shares eliminates non-systematic risk, i.e. risk incurred by returns uncorrelated with the return on a general share index. For fixed investments, the same approach suggests that managers should be unperturbed about the risk in specific markets, allowing shareholders to diversify their portfolios to balance this. However, the approach is severely qualified by unrealistic assumptions in regard to available information and zero costs of bankruptcy. Even more salient is the criticism that it is managers, not shareholders, who take fixed investment decisions.

The adoption of a managerial perspective, however, only qualifies the theory. It is still arguable that firms should carry out individual project appraisal in the context of the risk incurred for the entire set of the firm's investments. In other words, managers should estimate the marginal impact of project risk on the risk position of the entire assets of the firm. Put differently, systematic and unsystematic risk can also be defined at the level of the firm, and each project risk can be assessed in regard to both these components.

The adoption of the above theoretical framework in either its strong or its weak version world make it difficult to form any *a priori* expectation of the effect of increased total risk (systematic and unsystematic) on investment. It is only systematic risk, i.e. risk which cannot be diversified away, which requires a higher return to justify investment. For some large multinational companies, the risk of exposure in individual countries – represented, say, by GDP variability – may be largely unsystematic.

It may seem that models of risk and uncertainty have to distinguish between systematic and unsystematic risk. However, the merit of so doing is qualified by the observation that modern financial theory is not generally employed in fixed investment appraisal. Most firms appear to evaluate risk by looking at the total risk of each project in isolation from existing or proposed investments (Hull 1980, p. 114; Koutsoyiannis 1983, p. 630). One reason for this may be that there are in fact several sources of business risk: markets, prices, interest rates, exchange rates, productivity and competitor reactions. This makes the analysis of even project risk very complicated because the interaction of several stochastic variables has to be considered. Considering these issues, Reimann (1990) argues that managers are correct in distrusting risk-adjusted discount rates and that it is more approtiate to focus on variability of cash flow, i.e. business risk. The next section will look at the transmission mechanisms from business risk to investment behaviour. The categories of business risk given most attention will be those used in the empirical chapters later in the book, namely demand uncertainty and output price uncertainty.[1]

4.3   THE ROLE OF NON-LINEARITIES IN DECISIONS UNDER RISK

The effect of uncertainty on decisions occurs through various channels, but a number of these can be grouped together under the generic heading of non-linearities. The idea here is that the final objective of decision makers can be represented as a nested set of functions of the risky variable(s). Most commonly we are concerned with the expectation of the utility of profit, where profit is in turn a function of cost, price, output etc. Under certain (unusual) conditions, this expectation may be identical to the certainty value obtained by setting the stochastic variables equal to their mean. But in general, uncertainty makes the expected value different to this, owing to non-linearities in the profit function or in the function relating utility to profits. These non-linearities are more carefully described in the following, beginning with the non-linearity of the utility function – more commonly represented as risk aversion.

4.3.1   Risk aversion

Risk neutrality means that an agent is indifferent between a certain outcome and a fair gamble that has that outcome as the statistical expectation. The assumption of neutrality is convenient for theorizing (see later), but often it is more realistic to assume that the firm is averse to risk. Risk aversion can be represented as a concave utility function $U(\pi)$, where π is profits. The utility function is such that utility rises at a decreasing rate with the level of profits. The implication of this depends on the maximand of the firm. If the firm is maximizing the expected value of utility, it will prefer a certain outcome to a fair gamble which has that outcome as the expected result.[2] This follows from Jensen's inequality, illustrated in figure 4.1, from which it is clear that $U(E[\pi]) > E[U(\pi)]$.

The implications of risk aversion depend on the details of the model. However, a negative direction of influence will unambiguously arise from uncertainty in respect of stochastic variables such as output or output price if profits are linear or concave in these variables. Further results on risk aversion are given in appendix 4.1.

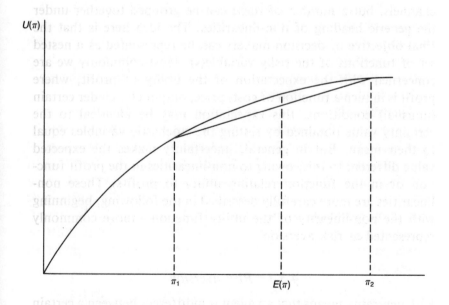

FIGURE 4.1   Risk aversion: $U(E[\pi]) > E[U(\pi)]$

4.3.2 Technological non-linearities

The concavity of the utility function is just a way of expressing risk-averse preferences. However, as may already be clear, utility of profits can also be concave in the determinants of profits without any recourse to risk aversion. It is therefore quite possible that expected profit maximization by a risk-neutral firm will lead to a different level of the decision variable under uncertainty than is implied by setting the stochastic variables to their expected values.

To see this, take a very simplified example where output Q is related to a capital flow I with a stochastic element representing variable productivity. Thus $Q^+ = Q(I) + e$, where e is a random variable symmetrically distributed with zero mean. Q is assumed to have positive but diminishing marginal products. Unit input cost is fixed at c and the output price is given exogenously as p. Expected profits are given by $E[\pi] = pQ(I) - cI$. This is maximized where $Q' = c/p$, giving the same I decision as under certainty. However, this result depends on the random component being such that $E[\pi(Q^+)] = \pi(Q)$. Now if we modify the formulation above just slightly, we destroy this result. Let the price now depend on production Q^+. It is now clear that taking expectations of profits over e will no longer necessarily give the equivalent result to the certainty case.

This example can be expressed quite generally by letting profits be a function of a decision variable Y and a stochastic variable X. For example, X might be demand and Y might be the level of an input or production. The formal condition for the level of the decision variable under uncertainty to be the same as under certainty is given by a formulation of the Rothschild and Stiglitz condition (Rothschild and Stiglitz 1971; Aiginger 1987). Specifically, the response of profits to the decision variable must be linear in the stochastic variable. In other words, π_Y must be linear in X.

If π_Y is concave, $\pi_{YXX} < 0$, Y is lower under uncertainty.
If π_Y is convex, $\pi_{YXX} > 0$, Y is higher under uncertainty.

Although difficult to grasp intuitively, the reasoning can be

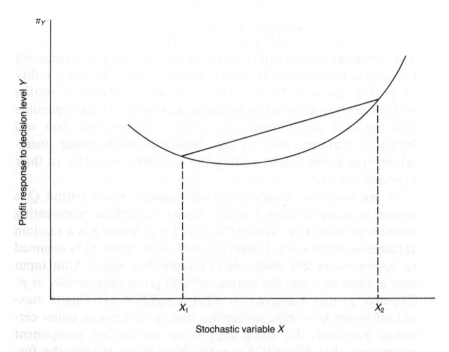

FIGURE 4.2 Rothschild-Stiglitz condition with convexity: $E_x[\pi_y] > \pi_y \mid x = E(x)$

made more transparent by a simple diagram showing how production might be greater under uncertainty.[3] In figure 4.2 the response of profits to the decision variable π_Y is graphed against the stochastic variable X for the convex case, i.e. $\pi_{YXX} > 0$. Any value of π_Y corresponding to a certain X will be lower than the expected value of π_Y corresponding to the uncertain X values obtained in a mean-preserving spread. Since the marginal profit is lower under certainty, the point of zero marginal profit will be reached sooner, i.e. with lower Y. The effect of uncertainty will be to induce greater Y.

The above condition, being fairly general, may be more difficult to follow than specific simple cases.[4] For example, if profits are linear in the stochastic variable, as in the simple example given earlier, the response of profits to the decision variable will be constant and the production decision will be the same under certainty and uncertainty.

4.4 DISEQUILIBRIUM MODELS

The effect of uncertainty is often analysed under the assumption that firms are continually engaged in *ex post* control to ensure profit maximization after the realization of the uncertain variable occurs. This kind of equilibrium modelling can apply equally well to cases of imperfect competition (where uncertainty is demand uncertainty) as to the perfect elasticity case (price uncertainty). Disequilibrium, however, may involve sticky price behaviour – commonly observed in industrial markets. The following model assumes price rigidity and draws on Aiginger (1987).

Writing Y for the decision variable – production – and X for stochastic demand, we can express the profit function as the difference of revenue r and cost c. In the certainty case, r and c are functions just of Y and the usual first-order profit-maximizing condition occurs, namely,

$$r'(Y) - c'(Y) = 0$$

Under uncertainty the production decision cannot be determined without some assumption as to how the disequilibrium between demand and production is resolved. The usual approach is to set the level of sales equal to the minimum of production, Y, or demand, X. The decision variable here is production, but in a slightly longer time framework it could be interpreted as capacity. Then

$$\pi = \min[r(X), r(Y)] - c(Y)$$
$$= Z - c(Y)$$

where

$$Z = \begin{cases} r(X) & \text{when } X < Y \\ \\ r(Y) & \text{when } X > Y \end{cases}$$

Let X have a probability density function $f(x)$ with a distribution function $F(x)$. Hence

$$E[Z] = r(X)f(x)\,dx + r(Y)f(x)\,dx$$
$$= r(X)f(x)\,dx + r(Y)\,(1 - F(Y))$$

$$dE[Z]/dY = r(Y)f(Y) + r'(Y)\,(1 - F(Y)) - r(Y)f(Y)$$
$$= r'(Y) - r'(Y)F(Y)$$

Thus

$$dE[\pi]/dY = r'(Y) - r'(Y)F(Y) - c'(Y)$$

It is easy to show that the second-order conditions are also satisfied.

The middle term in the last expression can clearly be construed as an extra cost term – the *marginal cost of uncertainty*. Thus the optimal level of output under uncertainty will be lower than under certainty.

It may seem counter-intuitive that such an unambiguous bias exists. However, it is the fixed exogenous price that ensures this; demand above the certainty production level is valued at zero because price equals the level of marginal cost under certainty, and this price is maintained in the uncertainty case.

Aiginger (1987) argues that this type of model gives 'the very strong result that optimal production will be lower under uncertainty as compared with certainty' (p. 37).[5] But this needs to be qualified once the marginal cost pricing assumption is relaxed. One alternative is the case of a fixed markup over variable cost. This model is then very similar to the 'newsboy' model (p. 68), and the result above applies as long as output price is less than twice unit variable cost, perhaps proxied by wage cost, i.e.

$$p < 2w$$

There is no reason to believe that this always holds, so occasionally this channel of influence could be expected to increase production under uncertainty. The qualification here would appear to correspond with what is commonly observed. Firms do not value at zero possible demand in excess of a certainty level.

In addition to the argument above, there are two further reasons which may qualify, though not displace, the theory of the marginal cost of uncertainty. Firstly, although the proposition as stated is true, it does *not* imply that an *increase* in uncertainty will always lead to a reduction in output. To see this we need merely note that the expression for expected profit maximization under uncertainty involves $F(Y)$, and the solution Y will be less than the certainty value of Y, Y_C. It follows that any change in $F(Y)$ at least beyond the value Y_C will have no effect on optimal Y. However, with a skewed distribution it is quite possible for the right hand tail to change shape while the left hand part of the distribution remains the same.

Another problem with the approach is that there are no cost penalties for failing to meet demand other than the associated loss in revenue. There is considerable evidence from work in industrial organization that market share can be lost permanently by the failure of timely production (Scherer 1986, chapter 4). The reported result is not robust to this consideration, as the latter implies an extra cost component which biases production upwards under uncertainty.[6]

To sum up this section, disequilibrium modelling is important because it conforms to what firms actually do. The implications for output or capacity are not entirely clear-cut, but a depressing effect of uncertainty could be presumed unless the inequality $p < 2w$ is unlikely to be true.

4.5 CAPITAL INPUT DECISIONS UNDER RISK

The above channels of influence apply to output decisions. The input decision is similar, but the issue here is complicated by the variety of possible models. Perhaps the most important new aspect is the need for multiperiod models, given that many capital goods have a dedicated purpose and negligible resale value. This is a separate question from the form of the production function (*ex ante* and *ex post*) which can also place restrictions on the firm's response to unanticipated out-turns. For example, the degree of substitutability may be important under price uncertainty because the realized conditions might imply an output produced with factor proportions different to the *ex ante* optimum.[7] The presence of scale economies or diseconomies may also affect the balance between the cost of too much capacity or not enough capacity to meet uncertain demand. Each of these cases may be

TABLE 4.1 Selected models of the capital input decision: effect of price or demand uncertainty under risk neutrality

Model	Restrictions						Effect of uncertainty on capital input
	1	*2*	*3*	*4*	*5*	*6*	
Lambert and Mulkay 1987	yes	no	yes	PC	yes	1	Negative unless very high profitability
Nickell 1978:5b	no	no	yes	CC	yes	1	Negative
Pindyck 1988	no	no	yes	CC	yes	2	Negative
Caballero 1991	no	no	yes	PP	yes	2	Negative unless asymmetry small
This text appendix 4.2	no	yes	yes	CC	yes	1	Negative
Kon 1983	no	no	no	PC	no	1	Negative for constant elasticity of substitution (CES) production
Caballero 1991	no	no	no	PP	yes	2	Positive
Nickell 1978:5d	no	no	no	PP	yes	1	Positive

Restrictions
These may apply only to part of the cited works.

1 Exogenous price assumed throughout.
2 Price decided *ex ante*, not varied subsequently.
3 Downward sloping demand curve assumed.
4 Putty-clay (PC) or clay-clay (CC) or putty-putty (PP) technology.
5 Asymmetrically large downward adjustment costs or capital irreversibility.
6 One- or two-period model (1 or 2).

analysed under price uncertainty or demand uncertainty. Furthermore, the results are sensitive to whether the form of demand uncertainty is multiplicative or additive. Demand uncertainty can also be analysed with fixed or flexible prices. It is therefore not surprising that the theoretical literature is replete with conflicting results.

Rather than offer a full survey of the models, it is proposed here to indicate a number of models which offer the strongest argument in favour of the direction of influence of uncertainty on investment being positive or negative. The main features of some selected models are set out in table 4.1.

4.5.1 Arguments for a positive direction of influence on investment

We begin with what we regard as the less likely result – a positive influence of uncertainty on investment. The models which demonstrate this effect are generally models of perfect competition with price uncertainty. Since these conditions only have a walk-on part in the play of life, the associated models are of only moderate interest. However, a positive influence of uncertainty on investment can also be derived under certain assumptions for fixed price models of demand uncertainty (Nickell 1978).

Price uncertainty leads to a higher capital input under perfect competition under some circumstances.[8] The argument here is based on the non-linearity effect discussed in section 4.3.2. The marginal profitability of capital is convex with respect to price for the given assumptions, and thus price uncertainty increases capital input (Nickell 1978; Abel 1983; Caballero 1991). Under perfect competition this result is robust to asymmetric costs of adjustment in dynamic models; perfect competition rules out any intertemporal effects. Whatever the price out-turn, the chosen first-period capital stock is irrelevant to the desired investment in later periods. However, as argued in section 4.5.2, the costs of irreversibility are not fully reflected in this framework, where they are limited to the costs of suboptimal factor combination.

The above models are based on non-linearities with price uncertainty. The same result – a positive influence of uncertainty on investment – could be obtained for a fixed price disequilibrium model if the inequality condition derived in section 4.4 is not satisfied. That result for production needs to be slightly modified to take account of the longer timeframe in which capital costs are distinguished from labour costs. Assuming that labour costs do not have to be incurred unless production takes place, but that capital has to be fully supported, the implication of this model is that the capacity Y^* chosen under uncertainty will be less than the decision under certainty if

$$i > (p - w)/2$$

where i, w and p are unit capital, labour and output price respectively (Nickell 1978, example 5a, p. 72; discussed also in Aiginger 1987, p. 84). This inequality may be written as

$$p < c + i$$

where $c = w + i$, the long-run marginal cost. The size of the markup reflects the value of forgone profits in the case of a stockout. The inequality may not be satisfied if the unit capital cost is low and if the markup is sufficiently high, i.e. in poorly competitive, labour intensive industries.

Thus, in this model the effect of uncertainty on the capital input decision depends on the size of the unit capital cost in relation to the unit net revenue $p - c$. Furthermore, the higher the markup for a given capital cost, the less likely it is that uncertainty will depress capital formation. Under risk neutrality, 'a firm is likely to introduce larger increases in capacity in response to uncertain demand increases if it expects high [profit markup] per unit' (Nickell 1978, p. 74). This is also the basis for the investment demand functions in Malinvaud (1983) and Lambert and Mulkay (1987).

4.5.2 Arguments for a negative direction of influence on investment

We now discuss what we regard as the more likely result – a negative effect of uncertainty. Risk aversion is probably the least contentious of the arguments supporting this. Most risk is systematic, i.e. it cannot be avoided by maintaining diversified portfolios (Nickell 1978; Reimann 1990). Empirical studies of managers' attitudes find in favour of risk aversion by firms at least in respect of large commitments (Aiginger 1987, appendix 5). This suggests that even if production decisions are taken under risk neutrality, most capital investment decisions are judged with risk in mind. Woods et al. (1985) find that payback methods of investment appraisal are more common in risky projects, suggesting that firms are risk-averse. Koutsoyiannis (1983) reports that many firms divide investments into risk classes, with much higher hurdle rates for projects in the highest risk class. Hull (1980) reports on managerial attitudes to risk which seem to focus strongly on the dispersion of net present value. McEachern and Romeo (1978) suggest that managers behave conservatively when there is no single dominant stockholder. Reimann (1990) reports evidence that risk seeking is largely a characteristic of lower-performing firms.

The asymmetry between possible *ex post* adjustment to capital and labour is another explanation for a negative effect of uncertainty on capital input. The adoption of the putty-clay assumption (factor proportions fixed *ex post*) with irreversible capital is one way in which this is modelled with respect to either price uncertainty (Kon 1983) or demand uncertainty (Lambert and Mulkay 1987). Under these conditions, flexibility is reduced with more capital intensive production.[9]

Other channels of influence are also likely to have a powerful effect. Although the possibility was raised in section 4.5.1 that the marginal cost of uncertainty could have a positive influence, this is exceptional, and the effect is likely to be negative for the normal range of markup and capital costs. Since the case of sticky prices is one of great empirical significance, this is probably one of the most important channels of influence operating.

The operation of this model, however, assumes that price is not only sticky but exogenous. A different model is discussed in appendix 4.2, where the price is set *ex ante* along with capacity under uncertain demand. This model also shows that capacity will be lower under uncertainty. The channel of influence here is the non-linearity of the profit function; price is set so as to equate the expected cost of stockout and overcapacity, and this is shown to be higher than the price under certainty.

The discussion above has largely concerned static models.[10] More recent literature has dealt specifically with the question of asymmetric costs of capital adjustment, including complete irreversibility in multiperiod models. Under irreversibility the investment rule is more stringent since there must be no state in subsequent periods in which current commitment would be regretted (in a probabilistic sense). Bernanke (1983) develops a model where the investor has a choice not only of project but also of its timing. He shows that under irreversibility and when information on project return is enhanced by waiting, postponing commitment will be desirable if improved information is more valuable to the investor than short-term return. Bernanke's model of 'investor caution' is thus an additional channel whereby uncertainty can have a retarding effect on investment. Other work along similar lines is developed in Pindyck (1988) and Bean (1989), and in appendix 4.3 to this chapter. Pindyck (1988) models investment under permanent uncertainty and argues that the usual net present value rule for investment is not valid since the cost of the firm's option to invest resources elsewhere is not considered: 'In many cases projects should be undertaken only when their present value exceeds twice their direct cost' (p. 969). Thus he argues for a negative effect of uncertainty on investment since the usual (positive) non-linearity effect with price uncertainty is more than offset by the increase in the value of the firm's option under uncertainty.[11] A slightly different model is presented in appendix 4.3. Firms are faced with mutually exclusive choices – either in respect of the timing of a single investment or between investments under capital rationing. It is shown that, under uncertainty, investment in any project will have a higher target rate of return than under certainty.

4.6 OLIGOPOLY AND PRE-EMPTION

Most of the literature on uncertainty deals with either perfect competition or monopoly. The interdependence of decision making means that oligopoly is a much more difficult object of study. Yet the vast proportion of industry output is accounted for by oligopolistic firms. Some forms of oligopoly with coordinated investment decisions can be considered as if capacity was determined by a monopolized industry, but this is not always the case (Paraskevopoulos et al. 1991).

The problem here is not an absence of theory but a surfeit. And Schmalensee (1988) has remarked that empirical research has 'failed to erase the impression that "anything is possible" left by the theoretical literature' (p. 676). Many game theory models now see investment as part of a two-stage investment-production game, but the results of these models are very sensitive to their chosen assumptions (Dixon 1986). The focus here then will be not on developing a new model but on surveying what the literature suggests about the effect of uncertainty on pre-emption, which is a possible feature of oligopolistic markets.

The question is whether uncertainty increases or decreases the likelihood of pre-emptive moves by firms and counter-steps by other firms. Spence (1979) suggests that uncertainty can be interpreted as raising investment cost even under risk neutrality. Although cautious about the implications, he appears to suggest that (demand) uncertainty would thus make rapid pre-emption less likely. This is supported in Tirole (1989, p. 321), but here the argument is that the incumbent excess capacity is expected to be higher under uncertainty. In any event the effect on investment modelled in these papers is only a partial equilibrium result. If uncertainty changes market structure we would expect this to have an effect on entry and investment.[12]

Porter and Spence (1981) report on an interesting coordination problem in the corn milling industry, where capacity to produce a sugar substitute will be built by up to eleven competitors. By assigning probabilities to different demand and sugar price scenarios, they simulate the actions of firms under the assumption of consistency, i.e. the assumption that expectations are consistent with the actual outcome implied by all competitors also having those expectation.[13] The simulation results show that risk to the firms (measured by the standard deviation of returns) rises sharply in most cases with higher investment under the most plausible probability distributions. This suggests that pre-emption is ruled out by high uncertainty: 'Unless firms lack an aversion to risk ... uncertainty will cause them to prefer and to choose lower levels of investment in the market' (p. 286). This result clearly depends on risk aversion. For risk neutrality, Porter (1983) suggests that uncertainty over future demand does not 'favour or disadvantage the leadership strategy' (p. 19). The probability of successful pre-emption is raised, but so too is the probability of excess capacity.

The case just considered illustrated the absence of pre-emption. By contrast, the following illustrates its occurrence. Ghemawat

(1984) reports a case study of the titanium dioxide industry, where firms are assumed to be characterized by large cost differences; this determines which firm attempts to pre-empt the other. The history of the industry from 1972 to 1977 accords with this assumption. 'Du Pont was the lowest cost producer and it thought that margins would be higher in the long run if it pre-empted and then exercised its market power to restrict output' (p. 155). In Ghemawat's model, cost differences helped to shape the industry structure. But the author makes clear that uncertainty could blur or overturn this result: 'Demand uncertainty acts as a great leveller in tending to equalize firms' costs and therefore their market shares' (p. 148). The argument here, as in Porter and Spence (1981), is based on risk aversion. The cheapest producer can avoid exposure to industry risk by cautious pre-emption by using the remaining high-cost producers as a buffer.

Finally, Gilbert and Lieberman (1987) show that pre-emption may only be effective in the short run with a longer-term tendency towards maintaining market shares. Thus, pre-emptive behaviour may be seen as a mechanism for ensuring investment stability in the face of uncertainty.

4.7 DECISION MAKING AND UNCERTAINTY

We have now surveyed some of the main channels of influence of uncertainty on firm decision making. This kind of theoretical work on the economics of uncertainty has yielded a rich menu of models; see, for example, the material surveyed in Hey (1979; 1981), Nickell (1978) or Aiginger (1987). There is considerable variety in the models concerned, both in respect of the initial assumptions – type of technology, role of adjustment costs, manner in which uncertainty occurs, flexibility of price etc. – and, in consequence, in respect of the conclusions on the likely effect of uncertainty. As we have seen, cautious investment behaviour will result from many forms of model, even under risk neutrality.

It is possible to apply empirical knowledge of economic behaviour from survey or econometric work so as to narrow down the range of models. But even if we could identify a canonical model of the economy, it would still be difficult to translate the model results into predictors of the effects of uncertainty. One reason for this is the coincidence of several forms of uncertainty that characterizes real time. In other words there may be considerable correlation between different indicators of uncertainty – output growth, price inflation, input cost etc. In most models of any complexity it is difficult enough to get unambiguous results in the presence of just one source of uncertainty. It might well need simulation techniques to tease out the possible interactions of simultaneously operating types of uncertainty.[14]

It is conceivable that such practical problems could be overcome with sufficient effort and that an economic model could be simulated with various sources of uncertainty to suggest optimal responses.[15] But again there may be more than one model, as when the extent of dependency between the model variables is in doubt. The complexity of the modelling required prompts the question of whether the models truly reflect the behaviour of decision makers. Simon (1979) has remarked that the important thing about satisficing theory as opposed to maximizing theory is that it 'showed how choice could actually be made with reasonable amounts of calculation and using very incomplete information' (p. 503). For companies who are regularly exposed to recognizable patterns of risk, the simulation approach will be used. But it cannot be regarded as a complete description of decision making, especially where the source of risk is shifting irregularly.[16]

There are compulsive arguments for why the actual decision-making arrangements of firms could not be based on the type of economic theory in section 4.3.2. Firstly, decision making in respect of future commitments is always an amalgam of bottom-up and top-down proposals. Only the former contain information on costs and productivity – and thus technological non-linearities. But the company board cannot confine its role to setting a target rate of return and allowing proposals to bubble up. Experience has shown that this will overstretch resources and that over-enthusiasm from below will cause excessive investment.[17] For this reason firms almost invariably practise a two-step procedure whereby first a budget is set, and then proposals which meet target return criteria at a lower level are prioritized within the constraint of the budget:

Instead of relying solely on an internal price mechanism to determine total capital expenditures, most corporations resort to some form of rationing, in which headquarters assigns budgets to the divisions without full knowledge of their opportunities. In some companies these budgets are inflexible. In others their use is part of a sequential process that still retains an element of a hurdle rate system.

(Taggart 1983, p. 1)

As the budget itself is often undertaken without the microknowledge of costs and productivity, economic theory has little to say about it; the usual theory of capital allocation under rationing assumes that detail on the alternative returns is available. Clearly the very setting of a budget – whether flexible or not – implies that some consideration is being given to questions such as exposure to debt and the overall strains on management that expansion brings. The budget setting process is partly intuitive and will reflect attitudes to risk in addition to those implicit in any risk-adjusted target rates handed down to the divisions. It seems clear that this method of decision making cannot take a great deal of account of the source of uncertainty, since it will only be vaguely known at board level how different sources are likely to affect profitability and the final effect will probably depend on the portfolio of projects selected.

It is not only in the budget decision that qualitative factors loom large. Pike (1982) shows that, for particular investment decisions, qualitative factors are important or very important according to 65 per cent of firms reporting. In the largest firms – those with capital budgets in excess of £50 million – these factors were 'very important' in nearly a quarter of the firms surveyed. Taking account of risk in such cases cannot easily be done in a formal manner. This may explain why only 37 per cent of firms surveyed in 1980 required a formal analysis of risk.[18] Among those who did assess risk, the methods were fairly evenly spread between three methods: sensitivity analysis; raising the target rate of return; and shortening the payback period. Only 12 per cent of firms went in for formal probability analysis.

Among the largest firms in 1980 nearly 80 per cent carried out sensitivity analysis, up from slightly over half such firms in 1975. But firms were obviously making use of more than one method of risk analysis in that the proportion of the largest firms shortening payback had also risen from a quarter to a third. Payback was used as a primary risk assessment in a quarter of the firms in 1980, and either payback or target rate adjustments were much more important as primary methods of risk assessment in all firms except the very largest.

It is not easy to relate these diverse practices to the economic theory discussed in the previous section. Firms adopting variable payback, for example, are not acting as risk-neutral profit maximizers. The only case where the decision maker could be said to be acting out the role implied by the formal models is where sensitivity analysis or probability analysis is carried out. If this were done so as to mirror the probability distribution of technical and market parameters, then at least the bottom-up part of the investment decision could be interpreted as reflecting the nuances of technological concavity in the production relationship or as reflecting the marginal cost of uncertainty. It appears, however, that although sensitivity analysis is used by the largest firms this is predominantly an industry-specific method, with only the chemicals/oils industry showing a majority for firms using this method and only a fifth of firms in the consumer durables industry employing the method. Furthermore, in order to approximate to the economic models, the use of sensitivity analysis would have to cover a large variety of alternative scenarios – rising by a power factor for each extra variable of interest. This does not now appear to be the practice even in the chemicals/oils business. Jefferson (1983) comments that the six scenarios produced at Shell UK in the early 1970s were excessive in number.

The overall impression then is one of predominant attention being given to subjective assessment, even at the bottom-up stage. As Pike (1982) notes: 'Managers appear to be reluctant to specify distributions of possible outcomes for each variable . . . and then to calculate the expected value' (p. 64). Among the reasons given for this were that marketing and production personnel did not seem able to quantify risk accurately; that risk was unconsciously taken into account; and that there was a danger of double counting by compounding the probability terms without knowing it.

Yet another consideration is the use which companies make of sensitivity studies. These studies are distinguished from probability assessments partly by the lack of necessity to ascribe to the underlying events any particular chance of occurrence. But frequently companies use the results to identify and avoid any serious risk. One response quoted in Pike (1982) suggests that a project has to be robust to a number of considerations, such as exchange rates and energy prices, before being accepted. Use of sensitivity analysis in this way will cause the convolution of different types of risk to become important, and again this is difficult to relate to the formal theory of the models. Furthermore, companies appear to sometimes manage risk by having a series of hoops for a project to go through – not just in terms of the sources of risk, but also in the methods of assessment of risk when multiple methods are used. This may be considered as a form of risk-averse behaviour but it is not readily amenable to formal analysis.

The focus on payback and shortening payback periods under heightened risk is important enough to merit some separate comment. Although frequently presented in elementary economics texts as having little justification, the use of payback may be rational from a mathematical programming point of view when interrelated projects are considered. If the company is capital rationed, future profitable projects may be constrained by internal finance, so a ranking of early commitments by payback will allow maximum flexibility for commitments to later projects. Put differently, shortening payback when capital investment is irreversible is a way of hedging against uncertainty.

This brief account of company decision making is sufficient to throw doubt on the effectiveness of channels of risk that are overly formal.[19] The most important channels probably involve *informal* (possibly unconscious) and *high-level* procedures. Some of the formal channels discussed in this chapter do qualify also on these scores, namely risk aversion and risk due to irreversibility. The marginal cost of uncertainty may also feature, though as noted above, this is likely to depend on the industrial characteristics of the investment. But there must be more doubt as to the effectiveness of the channel that has hogged the theoretical debate – the non-linearity of the technology.

4.8 CONCLUSIONS

There is no general model of the firm's investment decision under uncertainty. Risk aversion is just about the only mechanism which yields (fairly) general results, and even here it must be noted that risk aversion can interact with other channels of influence to exaggerate the bias to investment under uncertainty, whether that bias is up or down.

Despite this caveat, we have shown in section 4.5 the conditions under which a negative or a positive bias is more likely to occur. On the basis of these observations we have little doubt that the most common result is for demand uncertainty to depress investment, particularly under conditions of irreversibility. Oligopoly poses further problems, and the consensus here appears to be that pre-emption is less likely under uncertainty. Most of the chapter has been concerned with results that arise from the optimizing principle, though this has often been qualified by reference to price rigidity. The discussion in section 4.7 suggested that mechanisms based on non-linearity of the profit function could only be assumed to operate if companies were conducting formal sensitivity analyses.

Despite the lack of an unambiguous result – which is hardly unexpected – the material in this chapter gives an insight into the expected direction of influence of quantitative risk. Not all risks can be quantified, and we now press on in the next chapter to consider the case of uncertainty proper.

APPENDIX 4.1: RISK AVERSION IN ECONOMIC MODELS

A methodology for assessing the effects of risk attitude on the input decision is set out in Pleeter and Horowitz (1974). Writing

$$\pi = \pi(x_i), \quad i = 1,2,3$$

where x_1 is price, x_2 is output and x_3 is input, the decision on the input is arrived at by setting

$$\{E[U(\pi)]\}_{x_3} = 0$$

This implies

$$E[\{U(\pi)\}_\pi \, \pi_{x_3}] = 0$$

$$E[\{U(\pi)_\pi\}]E[\pi_{x_3}] + \text{cov}[1,2] = 0$$

where cov[1,2] is the covariance between the terms in brackets [].

For risk neutrality, $U(\pi)_\pi$ is a constant, so cov[1,2] = 0. With cov[1,2] < 0, a smaller input than the risk-neutral x_3 will be needed to restore the equality; Pleeter and Horowitz show that this is implied by the second-order conditions. What determines the sign of the covariance term? It is dependent partly on the concavity or otherwise of $U(\pi)$, i.e. on the attitude to risk, and partly on the specifics of the model. Pleeter and Horowitz show that for price takers – and with price as the random variable – cov[1,2] < 0 for risk-averse behaviour and capital input will be lower than under risk neutrality (p. 185). Other results can be determined using the same methodology.

Specific results for risk aversion were obtained by Nickell (1978) for a firm with flexible price and fixed coefficients technology facing an uncertain demand curve $aX(p)$, where a is a random variable. For the risk-averse firm, optimal capacity will always be lower than under certainty; furthermore, increasing risk aversion leads to a larger difference between the optimal capacities under certainty and uncertainty.

Nickell goes on to consider other models where substitution between inputs is possible. Here, as would be expected, the results are much less clear-cut. Input price (wage) uncertainty could cause a firm to have a higher capital stock to allow it the flexibility to respond to demand. But 'the flexibility provided by a large capital stock is less necessary to the firm which is able to increase output easily by simply intensifying the use of its capital stock by employing more labour' (p. 83). It can also be shown that for greater risk aversion the optimal capital stock *increases* for the flexible firm in order to insure it against high wages.

APPENDIX 4.2: INVESTMENT UNDER RISK WITH
INFLEXIBLE *EX ANTE* PRICES

It is relatively unusual for both price and capacity (or production quantity) to be considered as *ex ante*. This is surprising, as Aiginger (1987) suggests that such models (*p-q* models) are assessed by survey respondents to be among the most realistic (p. 165). Eichner (1976) also suggests that investment and price are linked decisions. The most comprehensive treatment of a model such as that proposed here is Karlin and Carr (1962). It is shown there that for a monopoly under multiplicative demand uncertainty, output price is always greater than under certainty. As will be indicated in the following, the uncertainty capacity may also be shown to be lower than certainty capacity.

Consider a stochastic demand function $ay(p)$, where p is price, y is expected demand and a is a stochastic parameter with lower bound of zero and density function $f(a)$. The firm maximizes expected profits but must choose capacity y^* and price before demand is known. Wage costs are negligible, and capital costs are c per unit of y^*.

The problem is

$$\underset{y^*, p}{\text{maximize}} \; E_a[\pi] \quad \text{where } \pi = pay - cy^*$$

Firstly:

If $a < y^*/y$ there is unused capacity.

If $a > y^*/y$ there is a stockout.

We have

$$E[\pi] = \int_0^{y^*/y} (pay - cy^*)f(a)\mathrm{d}a + (p - c)y^*(1 - F(y^*/y))$$

Partially differentiating this with respect to p and y^* using Leibniz's theorem and setting the derivatives equal to zero, we obtain after manipulation

$$y(1 + \epsilon) \int\limits_{0}^{y^*/y} af(a)\mathrm{d}a + y^*c/p = 0$$

where ϵ is the price elasticity of certainty demand. Some specific distribution for a is needed to obtain results.

It is shown in Driver et al. (1991) that for either a uniform or a log-normal distribution, the uncertainty price is indeed higher than the certainty price and the corresponding level of capacity formation is lower under uncertainty.

APPENDIX 4.3: THE EFFECT OF IRREVERSIBILITY ON INVESTMENT WITH RISK

This appendix simply formalizes a (possibly) intuitive idea that if you can invest *either* now (with a known return) *or* in a future period (with a stochastic return, revealed before commitment), then the more variable the future outcome, the higher the reservation level for pre-commitment in the present period.[20]

To see this, assume a planning horizon split into two periods. If an investment is made in period 1 it will, by assumption, exclude investment in period 2. It is shown in the following that greater variability of returns will make it more likely that the investment will be postponed.

The model is derivative of a classical dynamic programming problem in operational research – selling a car (Norman 1975, p. 18). With a fixed time horizon the seller has to decide whether to accept bids for the car, where the daily bids are identically and independently distributed $f(s)$; that is, the probability of a bid today between s and $s + \mathrm{d}s$ is $f(s)\mathrm{d}s$. The optimal policy is to accept a bid with n days left if the value of the bid V with n days left is greater than some critical value $V(n)$, where $V(0) = 0$ and

$$V(n + 1) = V(n) \int\limits_{0}^{V(n)} f(s)\mathrm{d}s + \int\limits_{V(n)}^{\infty} sf(s)\mathrm{d}s \qquad (4.1)$$

Note that $V(1)$ is the mean of s, i.e. $\bar{s}$. The reservation or minimum acceptable bid with one period left is simply the mean of the distribution of bids.

This result can be interpreted for the investment case as follows. The firm may invest in only one project because of capital rationing. Investment is possible at the beginning of the earlier or the later period. Profits from the earlier investment are assumed to be known – say because economic conditions over the project life are not liable to change. Profits from the later investment are stochastic with the known distribution $f(s)$, but the profit outcome is revealed at the beginning of the second period. If the earlier project is not accepted, the later one may be accepted if the revealed profit is acceptable according to the programming algorithm. Waiting further is also possible, but investment must take place by the end of the later period where the minimum acceptable profit is zero, i.e. $V(0) = 0$. We consider here only the decision to invest in the earlier period. $V(2)$ now refers to the minimum acceptable profits for the earlier investment to be accepted (with two periods to go), as determined by the programming algorithm.

The model can be used to consider the effect of uncertainty. From (4.1) we may write

$$V(2) = \bar{s} \int_L^{\bar{s}} f(s)\,ds + \int_{\bar{s}}^U sf(s)\,ds \tag{4.2}$$

where the lower and upper limits of the s distribution have been written as L and U respectively for greater generality, and where $F(L) = 0$ and $F(U) = 1$.

For the case of a symmetrical distribution, $V(2)$ increases with a mean-preserving spread of s if certain restrictive conditions are satisfied. To see this, write the second term in (4.2) as

$$\bar{s} - \int_L^{\bar{s}} sf(s)\,ds$$

Using integration by parts we obtain

$$\bar{s} - sF(s)\Big|_L^{\bar{s}} + \int_L^{\bar{s}} F(s)\,ds \tag{4.3}$$

Thus (4.2) may be written as

$$V(2) = \bar{s} + \int_L^{\bar{s}} F(s)\,ds \tag{4.4}$$

Under certain mean-preserving spreads the second term in (4.4) and thus the value of the whole expression (4.4) will increase. A restriction on the generality of the result is that weight must be added to the tails of the density function in such a way that the corresponding distribution functions only intersect once, i.e. at $s = \bar{s}$, the point implied by the symmetry condition. This condition is not overly restrictive; it merely rules out cases where the spread occurs by removing 'bites' from the middle of the distribution. Assuming the condition is satisfied, the minimum acceptable profit with two periods to go increases with a mean-preserving spread in s. Increased uncertainty thus increases the profit level needed to trigger pre-commitment.

We have thus shown that greater uncertainty in respect of profits from future investments will cause investment in the earlier period to require a higher minimum return to trigger pre-commitment. This is so irrespective of the origin of the uncertainty, e.g. whether it stems from price or output uncertainty.

NOTES

1 Investment equations are only disaggregated to industry level in the studies reported in this book. This means that the distinction between systematic and unsystematic risk is of less importance than for studies of more narrowly defined product lines.

2 For a consideration of other possible objectives under uncertainty, see Sugden (1987).

3 It is not always simple to apply the result where disequilibrium under uncertainty means that the profit maximization is being constrained, possibly inducing additional costs not incurred under certainty.

4 It is not really general because non-linearity can arise in many ways not considered, e.g. through the cost function.

5 He suggests that the reason why the result is not more frequently cited is that it relies on the price being the same under certainty and uncertainty, which may only be true in partial equilibrium models.

6 This point is discussed in relation to inventories in Aiginger (1987, pp. 68ff) and in Karlin and Carr (1962).

7 These complications arise even if we disregard the possibility of

uncertainty over factor prices. For a model of how uncertainty in
respect of factor prices influences the choice of capital input, see
Nickell (1978, pp. 80ff).

8 Caballero uses a Cobb-Douglas production function. Hartman (1976)
shows that a higher elasticity of substitution or large diseconomies
of scale could favour a lower capital input, for the obvious reason
that increased output under a higher realized price either would be
less profitable or need not be produced in such a capital intensive
manner. Kon (1983) also obtains the possibility of a lower capital
input under uncertainty, partly by ruling out an *ex post* increase in
the labour–capital ratio.

9 The argument here is that labour can be laid off in a recession while
machines cannot (Black 1968, p. 311). John Harvey Jones recently
pointed to the continuing relevance of this: 'Because they [progressive
firms] have invested in modern equipment, labour costs have already
been heavily reduced, so that further redundancies are of little help.
Meanwhile, the burden of their capital costs remains' ('Why UK
firms will limp into Europe', *The Observer*, 28 April 1991).

10 A good account of how static models carry over into dynamic ones
is given in Nickell (1978), which deals with models of the dynamic
capacity path under demand uncertainty with delivery lags. The
latter cause firms to anticipate uncertain changes in demand, thus
smoothing the capacity path. Nickell shows that the outcomes of
the static models generally carry over into the dynamic ones in that
uncertainty tends to lower the optimal capacity path. The result is
strengthened under irreversibility.

11 In Caballero (1991) the negative influence on investment is rather
muted – at most a few percentage points – for a simulation with
demand elasticity of 2.5 and a ratio between the costs of downward
and upward adjustment of 1 to 50. This, however, is in the context
of a model of price flexibility and full utilization of capacity, where
the costs of irreversibility stem from the necessity of suboptimal
factor proportions. This reinforces the distinction drawn in Aiginger
(1987) between petty and severe uncertainty. The former describes
cases where there is significant *ex post* control, muting the effect
of uncertainty. By contrast, putty-clay models, with the possibility
of underutilization of capital, or models with exogenous price
exhibit severe uncertainty effects due to disequilibrium.

12 Porter and Spence (1981) suggest that concentration is a U-shaped
function of risk. Pleeter and Horowitz (1974) also discuss market
structure and risk, and suggest that collusion will be a feature of
uncertain circumstances.

13 Although defended vigorously by Porter and Spence, this assumption is often ungrounded. See the discussion of naphthalene in Foster (1986) or the case study material in Freeman (1982). On the other hand, Sarantis (1978) has shown that concentrated industries have more stable investment behaviour than unconcentrated ones, allowing for other variables such as capital intensity. This suggests that some form of coordination may commonly be practised.

14 As an example of this, consider the introduction of the European single market in 1992. Not only does this involve the reduction in tariffs and quotas which can be expected to lead to greater trade; it also involves the removal of non-tariff barriers even in non-manufacturing areas, and furthermore encourages the movement of labour and capital across the boundaries of the national states. The end result is to reduce transaction costs and factor costs by easing administrative burdens and by structural adjustment. But the problems of structural adjustment are also to be dealt with by greater public support for regional or technological activity. It should be apparent that several sources of uncertainty are operating.

15 A good account of the complexity involved in using probability analysis for assessing multiple sources of uncertainty is given in Lutz and Lutz (1951, chapter 15.3). Hull (1980) reports on the practical implementation of sensitivity studies with dependencies between the stochastic variables. He suggests that failure to take account of full dependencies could have a large effect on the dispersion of net present value, though he does not discuss the effect on the mean.

16 The argument here is different from that sometimes advanced that economic theory is simply too complicated for businessmen to understand. The human being, after all, is capable of very complicated calculations in performing even minor tasks. Crossing the road, for example, appears to involve the brain in integrating over the speed and acceleration of cars. But the point about these operations is that they are repetitive. It is in connection with uncertain situations where there is a fair degree of uniqueness that we must doubt the ability of the decision maker to perform like a complex machine.

17 Freeman (1982) quotes work by Edwin Mansfield which shows development costs of technological improvements to be about twice those originally estimated. He also quotes work showing that even where engineers have financial incentives to make accurate predictions, they underestimate costs, partly because they feel that they have a better perception of likely successes than more senior

management (p. 153).

18 This figure varied from 25 per cent in the smallest-firm category to 61 per cent in the largest-firm category (1980 figures). The latter figure had increased from 44 per cent in 1975.

19 Pindyck (1988) notes that managers do not seem to use 'correct' formal methods to take account of risk, but 'use the wrong method to get close to the right answer' (p. 983).

20 This links with the precautionary motive for liquidity. As Chick (1983) notes: 'Keynes stressed the desirability of having extra money to take advantage of unexpected bargains' (p. 196).

5

Uncertainty: Conceptual Issues and Measurement Problems

5.1 INTRODUCTION

The previous chapter has shown how investment might respond to variation in risk, where that was understood to involve a known distribution of future outcomes. Arguably, real business decisions are often made in an environment where a simple risk calculus is not possible. Perhaps the probabilities are unknown or the exhaustive listing of contingencies is not possible. In such cases the issue of concern is uncertainty – a broader notion than that of risk. The question then arises of whether any theoretical perspective is possible on investment under uncertainty.

In this chapter we discuss some conceptual issues in regard to uncertainty. While we have no wish to be overly exegetical or to champion any particular historical view as correct, it nevertheless is true that we can learn from past debates about the nature and significance of uncertainty. In particular we can appreciate why economists have tended to avoid the area of applied work on uncertainty, given the nature of the difficulties.

The discussion of risk and uncertainty inevitably leads into philosophical issues about probability and knowledge. We can simplify the discussion by using a version of a matrix categorization developed by Lawson (1988), as in table 5.1. This matrix is useful both in avoiding confusion and in delimiting the focus of discussion. We will be concerned in sections 5.2 and 5.3 only with elaborating on views which involve unmeasurable probability. This rules out the rational expectations school, which avoids the problem of uncertainty and assumes an identity between

TABLE 5.1 Probability/uncertainty categorization matrix

	Probability is a property of belief	*Probability corresponds to external reality*
Uncertainty corresponds to a situation of numerically measurable probability	Subjectivists (including Bayesians	Rational expectations school
Uncertainty corresponds to a situation of numerically unmeasurable probability	Keynes	Knight (?)

subjective (measurable) probabilities and the 'underlying' objective distribution. The discussion also avoids subjectivism, though the effective distinction between this view and that of Keynes is not clear-cut (Gillies 1973, p. 24; but see also Davidson 1991). It will merely be remarked here that subjectivists consider all probability statements only to have meaning as personal beliefs, and thus no distinction is generally drawn between risk and uncertainty.[1] The intention of the next few sections is to explore the remaining differences in the approach to uncertainty so as to come to a better understanding firstly of its likely effects and secondly of how it might be captured by some quantitative proxy.

Section 5.2 surveys Keynes' views, particularly on the frequency approach to probability. Section 5.3 suggests the need for a theory of simple rules. This leads on to a consideration of such a theory in section 5.4. The implications of this for investment are discussed in section 5.5. Section 5.6 introduces some problems in measuring uncertainty. Section 5.7 argues in favour of the dispersion measure. This measure is defended against the alternative of forecast error in section 5.8.

5.2 KEYNES, KNIGHT AND UNCERTAINTY

In chapter 12 of *The General Theory*, and in subsequent writings,

Keynes presented a view of investment behaviour as driven by volatile fears and hopes. Analysis of the investment decision could only be partial because the forces of uncertainty, as distinct from risk, were incapable of quantitative analysis. Agents must act capriciously because there is no rational basis for exact judgement. The trouble with this argument is that the lack of a rational premise for action can also justify the importance of convention – the opposite of caprice – in human decision making. And there seems no basis for judging which of these outcomes – convention or caprice – will be dominant at any time. Keynes emphasized the notion of caprice when he wished to point to the volatility – and therefore 'autonomy' – of investment. But convention too was important, e.g. in explaining interest rate expectations, or as a basis for explaining speculative stock market bubbles. Keynes invoked psychological reasons to explain why convention would generally dominate over caprice (Winslow 1989, p. 1180). These are important insights, but they are not fully developed in Keynes and repay further analysis.

One interpretation of the distinction between (measurable) risk and (unmeasurable) uncertainty as used in economics is traced to Knight (1971) and Keynes (1973, vols VIII, VI and XIV). If the probability distribution of future returns could be calculated, risk analysis could allow for a form of calculation based on expected returns. But in the case of some events, it is possible that the basis for calculating the probability distribution does not exist.

For Keynes, writing in the *Treatise on Probability*, 'a numerical measure can actually be obtained in those cases only in which a reduction to a set of exclusive and exhaustive equiprobable alternatives is practicable' (1973, vol. VIII, p. 70). Keynes also argued that even where 'probabilities' could be numerically defined, any probabilistic judgement was only one dimension of a two-dimensional phenomenon. One also had to discuss the confidence or 'weight' attached to any probabilistic judgement. Comparisons between probabilities may thus be impossible.

Keynes' views on probability were originally published in the same year (1921) as Knight's major work, and neither cites the other's text.[2] Nevertheless some similarities are evident from Knight's remark that 'the practical difference between the two categories, risk and uncertainty, is that in the former the distribution of the outcome in a group of instances is known, while in the case of uncertainty this is not true, the reason being in general that it is impossible to form a group of instances, because the situation dealt with is in a high degree unique' (p. 233).

Now Keynes was not, at least at this stage, a frequentist, and probability for him was epistemic rather than an aspect of external reality. Nevertheless he had occasion to remark that 'if we knew that our material could be likened to a game of chance, we might expect to infer chances from frequencies with the same sort of confidence as that with which we infer frequencies from chance' (1973, vol. VIII, pp. 419–20). It is in this sense that we can put Keynes and Knight on the same footing. There is, however, a difference between them. Knight argues that we can nearly always infer chances from frequencies because in practice there is no such thing as a unique event: 'To say that a certain event is contingent or "possible" or "may happen" appears to be equivalent to saying that "such things" have been known to happen before ... Insurance deals with those [contingencies] which are "fairly" classifiable' (1971, pp. 246–7).[3] And even where no objective basis exists for computing objective probabilities, Knight allows for the possibility of (subjective) measurable probability judgement (Lawson 1987, p. 51).[4] Knight thus appears to have anticipated Coddington's objection to Keynes' well known remarks giving instances of uncertainty as 'the prospect of a European war ... or the price of copper and the rate of interest twenty years hence' (1973, vol. XIV; quoted in Coddington 1982, p. 481). For Coddington, as for Knight, these do not form a category totally distinct from other events that are more easily assessed in terms of probability.

Keynes' approach is far less compromising. He implicitly defines uncertainty as the case where there is no basis whatever upon which to form any calculable probability: 'No method of calculation, however impracticable, has been suggested' (1973, vol. VIII; quoted in Lawson 1985, p. 914). The case that Keynes was discussing was leading up to this extraordinary statement concerning a person calculating the probability of rain: 'If the barometer is high, but the clouds are black, it is not always rational that one should prevail over the other in our minds, or even that we should balance them' (1973, vol. VIII, p. 32). Now it is interesting that the discussion here concerns two separate influences on probability which are difficult to measure or reconcile. It is not the case that the probability set is not closed; indeed, it appears to contain only two elements, 'rain' and 'not rain'. Nor is it the case that the *event* is unique. The objection to being able ever to measure probability concerns the difficulty in combining strands of evidence. And, of course, the different strands of evidence will always create a unique relationship between the observer and the evidence. In arguing this, Keynes does not deny that 'our conclusions would have a numerical probability, relative to slightly different premises' (p. 35). Thus, Keynes conceptualized uncertainty as arising from a difficulty in combining fragmentary evidence. This contrasts with a common interpretation of Keynes which stresses the unique nature of economic events.

Later in the *Treatise on Probability*, Keynes discusses the difficulties of combining strands of information by elaborating on the concept of the 'weight' of the evidence. The concept can be illustrated (though Keynes does not do so) by returning to the example of assessing the likelihood of 'rain'. How does one (rationally) compare and combine the information or probabilities of rain given by the barometer and the black cloud, other than in terms of the weight attached to these pieces of evidence that is provided by background information, e.g. barometers are generally reliable but tend to stick, and assessment of cloud is a difficult matter? The two pieces of probabilistic evidence are difficult to combine because they have different weights or reliabilities.

This emphasis on non-formal reasoning underpinned much of Keynes' later writing. And the underlying explanation seems to be consistent: strands of evidence are difficult to compare and combine. For example, there is an explicit reference to the concept of evidential weight in chapter 12 of *The General Theory*: 'By "very uncertain" I do not mean the same thing as "very improbable"; cf. my *Treatise on Probability*, chapter 6, on "The Weight of Arguments" ' (1973, vol. VII, p. 148).[5] This emphasis on non-formal reasoning survives Keynes' rejection of the theory of probability in the *Treatise* in favour of a form of frequency theory (Winslow 1989, p. 1177).

However, for some writers, and occasionally for Keynes, uncertainty is defined in a more radical sense than lack of well defined probabilities. Uncertainty reflects a choice set that is not closed or is shifting too rapidly, as a result of either thought, interaction or external conditions: 'At the moment of choice, the individual will have conceived of a certain number or range of possibilities. Nevertheless, he is fully aware that in a world of change, something might happen that he could not list beforehand. So he perceives his set as, in principle, unbounded' (O'Driscoll and Rizzo 1985, p. 66).

Now whichever of these sources of uncertainty – combinations of vague probabilities or the lack of a closed choice set – is involved, it undermines the case for a purely formal assessment of risk. These objections stand even if we agree with Knight and Coddington that in practice one rarely encounters unique events.

This negative conclusion, however, begs the question of how decisions are actually made. It is unfortunate that Keynes, who knew the limitations of formal risk analysis, did not address in any detail the procedures that decision makers would evolve to deal with choice under uncertainty.

5.3 THE PROCESS OF DECISION

It would be possible to dichotomize investment decisions by contrasting 'normal times' when appropriate probabilities or risk analyses could be carried out, and 'abnormal times' when true uncertainty makes risk calculus impossible. It is doubtful, however, if this dichotomy has much validity. Even in normal times, events may be too complex to allow for a comprehensive accounting for possible outcomes.[6]

Even with known probabilities, decision makers face great difficulty in applying economic theory; this is clear from the existing plethora of models of decision making under risk (Hey 1979; Nickell 1978; Aiginger 1987). In many of the models considered by Nickell (1978), for instance, the response of a risk-neutral investor to uncertainty of various kinds cannot be signed even after many assumptions and algebraic essays. And these models are among the more simple on offer. It seems therefore that the existence of complex forms of risk implies the existence of uncertainty. Indeed, Hey (1979) himself has accepted these points and argued that 'a new approach may give results that essentially consist of justifications of the *ad hoc* rules that people actually appear to use in practice' (p. 233).[7]

A theory of these rules and procedures was recently put forward by Ronald Heiner (see section 5.4). In assessing this theory it is important to bear in mind that it explicitly uses a frequentist approach in the Knightian sense of a practical grouping of instances. In this sense its starting point is somewhat different from that of the early Keynes. Yet, at least by 1931, Keynes had come round to the view that 'degrees of belief and "induction" are based upon "mental habits" whose analysis belongs to "human" rather than formal logic' (Winslow 1989, p. 1178). This being the case, there can be little quarrel with an analysis which simply reflects the fact that human logic involves reactions learned from the practical groupings of instances.

5.4 THE ORIGIN OF CONVENTION

In a series of papers, Heiner (1983; 1985a; 1985b; 1985-6; 1986) has developed a theory of decision making where uncertainty arises owing to a lack of perception or execution skills on the part of the agent. This involves what Heiner terms a competence-difficulty gap (C-D gap). According to this theory, the agent will ignore even freely available information if the reliability ratio (the ratio of the chance of correctly responding under the right circumstances to the chance of mistakenly responding under the wrong circumstances) is less than a tolerance level (the ratio of the posterior expected gain to expected loss).

It is instructive to apply this theory to Keynes' illustrative example of decision faced with the possibilities that it will rain or be fine. We define the following:

h posterior probability that it will be fine
L average loss arising from taking avoiding action when it will
   be fine

G average gain arising from taking avoiding action when it will rain
r probability of correctly recognizing indications of rain
w probability of mistakenly believing that rain will occur.

The probability of the right condition for taking avoiding action is therefore $1 - h$, the probability of rain.

For it to be appropriate to take avoiding action, we must have the reliability ratio greater than the tolerance level:

$$r/w > Lh/G(1 - h) \tag{5.1}$$

If a new climate were to evolve in which much lighter rain were to become normal, with associated lower gain from taking avoiding action, the reliability ratio would have to reach a higher minimum limit. In general the only way for the reliability ratio to rise for a given C–D gap is for the information to be acted on less frequently (Heiner 1986). This is the origin of convention.

Heiner (1985b) defines uncertainty as arising in those cases in which $r < 1$ and $w > 0$ (p. 393). Uncertainty, therefore, does not necessarily imply 'risk' , since the outcomes could in theory be non-stochastic.

If we define *risk* as the variance of the distribution of outcomes, it is clear that reliability and risk are not always simply related. Reliability refers to the likelihood of the agent recognizing the right conditions for selecting a particular action, while risk involves the distribution of outcomes. To take an example, a colour blind person predicting that the roulette ball will stop at red will have a lower reliability than a colour sighted person, even though the associated 'risks' will be the same.[8]

Heiner provides a rationalization for Keynes' view that a simple probability or risk calculus is inadequate: personal uncertainty interacts with objective probability. For Keynes, 'in almost all everyday arguments of any degree of complexity, an elaborate combination of induction and analogy is superimposed upon a narrow and limited knowledge of statistical frequency' (1973, vol. VIII, pp. 118–19). Heiner's advance is to provide a rational explanation of how 'induction and analogy' are used to guide decisions by judging the associated reliability. Action will be avoided unless reliability exceeds a given threshold. His approach also explains how *convention* arises, as a product of excluding complex considerations, and how variation about convention is possible owing to different C–D gaps.[9]

To the question posed at the outset – whether convention (i.e. conservatism) or caprice would be the outcome of increased uncertainty – Heiner provides an equivocal answer. In general convention will dominate, though the meaning of that term needs to be further explored in the next section.[10]

5.5 INVESTMENT AND CONVENTION

One implication of Heiner's theory is that decision makers react to uncertainty by reducing the probability of responding to new information. Applied to investment theory, this might seem to indicate that investment would become less volatile under increased uncertainty. Taken as it stands, this does not appear to offer a view of the direction in which investment would be affected by uncertainty. If the decision variable is gross investment, this will always be positive so that greater stability might often imply cutbacks. On the other hand, it is possible to argue that a greater uncertainty in respect of a forecast downturn might cause investment to be maintained. This is the position of Gowdy (1985–6) who infers a greater macroeconomic stability from heightened uncertainty.[11]

In Heiner's (1983) own view, greater uncertainty will 'constrain behaviour to simpler, less sophisticated patterns which are easier for an observer to recognize and predict' (p. 570). It is evident that this would imply a focus on shorter-term effects and favour liquidity over commitment. Thus, the balance of the argument seems to point to increased uncertainty exerting a downside influence on investment rather than simply freezing existing decisions and decision patterns.[12]

This view is reinforced by a consideration of the likely information filters that come into play as reliability deteriorates. Information which is 'distant' or 'non-local' tends to be disregarded. Distance in this context can refer to distance ahead in time (favouring short payback); distance from previous behaviour patterns (favouring inflexible response); or distance in the sense that the outcome depends on the interaction of non-local agents. Thus the notion of 'convention' is here extended to encompass a broader range of possibilities than merely maintaining previous behaviour (Heiner 1986, pp. 82–4; Lawson 1987, p. 969). The conclusion of this discussion is that uncertainty in the Heiner sense will bias input decisions downward if irreversibility applies. In this case the required decision is not only an input decision, but the forfeit of an option as well (Pindyck 1988). The reliability condition applied to the latter will probably be the binding one, and this will tend to have a negative effect on capital input. The conclusion that irreversibility is the crucial feature which biases investment downward complements the same conclusion reached by Aiginger (1987) in respect of investment under calculable risk. 'Petty uncertainty' is distinguished from 'severe uncertainty' by the extent to which *ex post* correction or control is possible (p. 103).

5.6 PROBLEMS IN THE MEASUREMENT OF UNCERTAINTY

Any quantitative investigation of the effect of uncertainty on investment requires a measure of uncertainty. Heiner and (sometimes) Keynes argue that uncertainty arises owing to human difficulties of perception and information processing. Clearly uncertainty can be related at a personal level to the reliability ratio associated with particular sets of managerial actions, e.g. speculating on currency movements or diversifying into new product areas. Zero uncertainty would imply that the agent never chooses an action when it is wrong to do so; this corresponds to an infinite reliability. A reliability of one would imply a complete inability to distinguish the right from the wrong conditions for action. But, even if reliability were observable – it is not – it still could not be used as a *measure* of uncertainty or decision-making difficulty.

Reliability is defined independently of the probability of the 'right' circumstances for action. This is an important source of difference between reliability (or its absence) and another indicator of uncertainty – forecast error. Forecast error concerns predictive accuracy about *actual* out-turns, whereas reliability is concerned with predictive accuracy of (objectively influenced) perceptions of what *might* happen. These perceptions may bear a complex relationship to past out-turns and forecasts.[13] Thus, a macroeconomic forecaster might be able to track very well the normal performance of the economy but be a poor predictor of turning points. In this case low reliability, in the sense of poor capacity to notice turning points, might coincide with good forecasting performance if turning points (the 'wrong' circumstances) occurred infrequently.

In fact, neither reliability nor forecast error is a good summary statistic for decision-making difficulty. The former ignores the distribution of outcomes – risk – and represents only one aspect of decision-making difficulty. The consequence of this is that there is no absolute measure of a reasonable reliability ratio. If the right conditions scarcely ever happen then the reliability must be near infinite for the action to be possibly selected. On the other hand, if the right condition occurs nearly always, a low reliability will suffice for the action to be considered.[14] The near infinite reliability for rare actions is a reason why such possibilities tend to be discounted, and this is a feature of convention (Heiner 1983, p. 567; Heiner 1988, p. 152). It appears, therefore, that reliability is not a good index of decision-making difficulty. What is more relevant for decision making is *reliability in relation to the tolerance level*. But again, this has the disadvantage of being incapable of measurement.[15]

The alternative measure of some summary of forecast errors is also flawed. Forecast errors are indicators of decision difficulty only in so far as successive period out-turns are realizations from a common statistical distribution which mirrors the probability distribution for the current out-turn.[16]

5.7 DISPERSION AS A MEASURE OF UNCERTAINTY

One intuitively appealing measure of uncertainty is the dispersion of forecasts across informed agents.[17] The following discussion is intended to argue the merits of this.

Let the knowledge in regard to a particular event be built up by sampling from a number of information sources. These sources are then weighted by forecasting agents. If the same sources are consulted by all agents and each is perfectly accurate, there should be unanimous agreement on a point forecast, and indeed on the entire probability distribution of the outcome if it is stochastic. This corresponds to the previously discussed case of perfect reliability for all agents with the additional assumption of perfect information.

A diversity of point estimates is explainable either by differential access to information or by differential capability of processing information. Once either of these is admitted, dispersion of point estimates is possible. Dispersion, then, implies personal uncertainty.

However, a concern with personal uncertainty takes us only so far; we also have to form an opinion of what 'social' uncertainty is if we are to apply the concept in a macroeconomic framework. An extreme view would be that it is sufficient for one agent to be perfectly reliable and informed for zero uncertainty to prevail. But this can be rejected if we introduce the question of how such an individual would be recognized or if we place limits on the scope of the individual's activities.

Ideally a measure of social uncertainty would be a weighted index of personal uncertainties (however measured) with weights perhaps reflecting these uncertainties. Lacking this, we might restrict ourselves to a small number of well informed (equally informed) agents. We then form some average of their uncertainty.

The above is one method of conceptualizing social uncertainty as built up from individual uncertainties. But this may be an unnecessary formalization. Group uncertainty may have a meaning outside individual uncertainty. Suppose at a board meeting each member is asked for an opinion. The group uncertainty may be formed not as an average of personal uncertainties but by noting the dispersion of the replies, i.e. the point estimates, suitably weighted to accord with *a priori* judgements or the track record of advice.

The latter measure is really an inverse measure of consensus rather than uncertainty. However, there are theoretical and empirical reasons to believe that personal uncertainty (appropriately defined) and lack of consensus are correlated.

To see this, recall what has been argued to generate the dispersion of point estimates of forecast variables. Assuming equal access to information, the dispersion will reflect differential C–D gaps and reliabilities.[18]

The reliability of agents is a function of the complexity of the environment. Heiner (1986) remarks that 'Uncertainty increases as either perceptual abilities become less effective, or the environment becomes less predictable, or both' (p. 70).[19] It is the complexity of the environment that is of interest here. As this varies, individuals both become less certain *and* respond to source information with a variety generated by their differential capacity to handle information.[20] In short, both the average of personal uncertainties and the dispersion of the point estimates should vary together as the environmental complexity varies.[21]

Empirical work gives some support for the hypothesis above if we are prepared to take the liberty of equating personal uncertainty with the subjective estimate of variable ranges. The connections between point forecast dispersion and average personal uncertainty have been investigated in an important study by Zarnowitz and Lambros (1987), though they do not motivate their work with reference to the Heiner framework. These authors made use of the US National Bureau survey data, which contain individual measures of perceived uncertainty (as represented by forecast ranges) on output and prices as well as point estimates for each respondent. Using these data, the authors were able to examine the correlation between sets of dispersion indicators (cross-section standard deviation) and average personal uncertainty (the mean of individual standard deviation of expectations).[22] The results are too rich to be described in detail, but the authors' conclusions are that although dispersion tends to understate subjective risk and to show greater variability over time, nevertheless measures of consensus and risk are for the most part positively correlated: 'There is some direct empirical support here for what is often taken for granted, namely that greater interpersonal differentiation of expectations is a symptom of greater uncertainty' (p. 607).[23]

To conclude this section, we may note that diversity can be generated either by differential competence or by differential access to information. The latter notion can be linked to a Bayesian interpretation where greater information will allow greater convergence. This is not necessarily inconsistent with the Heiner view if greater information reduces environmental complexity and also generates greater convergence.[24]

5.8 UNCERTAINTY VERSUS DEFICIENT FORESIGHT

The Heiner concept of uncertainty implies that agents can be uncertain even when their forecasts are repeatedly correct for a finite number of periods. This concept contrasts with the notion of uncertainty as deficient foresight, as suggested by Coddington (1982). Coddington observes that, for Keynesian theory, it is not the fact of uncertainty that is important but rather how individuals are supposed to respond to uncertainty. However, he himself does not appear to accept an analysis on the level of behavioural response. For if indeed it is the response to uncertainty that is of interest, there seems little point in defining uncertainty in relation to some objective (and future) truth. Nevertheless this is what he does: 'One would not be at all happy in expounding a theory in which everyone could – repeatedly – be perfectly confident one moment and discover themselves to have been wrong the next. So it is to the second idea of certainty as correct foresight that we are driven' (p. 483).

Now if uncertainty is viewed as determining decisions, it is unclear why these have to be validated *ex post* except in so far as errors feed back on expectations. To take an example, there was a good deal of agreement among UK investment managers in 1980, following the introduction of the Medium-Term Financial Strategy, that inflation would be reduced to quite low levels. As it turned out, these managers had systematically to revise their expectations over the next five quarters, having seriously underpredicted it (Taylor 1987). But the degree of agreement may have indicated a state of low uncertainty which could be expected to have influenced behaviour. Equally well, there may be periods in which forecast errors are low but uncertainties great.[25]

5.9 CONCLUSIONS

Uncertainty attends risk, and attempts to deal with this simply on the basis of probability axioms have limited validity. As noted by Hey (1983), real life problems are beyond the computational power of the decision maker: 'The economics of uncertainty must abandon its preoccupation with optimal rules of behaviour and concentrate instead on reasonable rules of thumb' (p. 139). This observation was prescient, as it foreshadowed the development of Heiner's theory, which attempted to analyse uncertainty in a different way from traditional optimization. Such an approach can explain convention, a feature that Keynes repeatedly emphasized in his writing on decision making under uncertainty but for which he failed to provide an adequate theory.

The concept of a conventional response is not transparent. However, it was argued earlier that in response to heightened uncertainty a downward bias in capital input is more likely than inflexible response, at least under irreversibility.

Heiner's theory also leads to an understanding of how environmental complexity can simultaneously affect personal uncertainties and the dispersion of estimates across agents. No measure of uncertainty is without ambiguities and difficulties, but it has been argued that the dispersion of forecasts is a sensible indicator. The meaning of this measure is further explored in the following chapter, where empirical measures of dispersion for the UK are also presented.

Finally, it should be stressed that although the arguments mentioned above point to a negative influence of uncertainty on capital investment, nothing in the theory suggests any particular functional form for that relationship. The theory is similarly silent on the strength of the putative relationship.

NOTES

1 Stigler remarks in the preface to Knight (1971) that 'tradition has assigned a distinction between risks (capable of actuarial treatment) and uncertainty (stochastic events not capable of such treatment) . . .

modern analysis no longer views the two classes as different in kind' (p. xiv). Davidson (1991) qualifies this view of subjective probability.

2 Although not published until 1921, the *Treatise* was mostly written at least a decade earlier. There is considerable debate on whether the philosophical basis of Keynes' writings shifted from 'atomic' to 'organic' by the time the connections between probability, uncertainty and growth were more cogently formulated in the 1930s (see Lawson 1985; Hamouda and Smithin 1988; Davis 1989; Winslow 1989).

3 Knight (1971) notes elsewhere that Lloyd's takes bets, for example, on a royal coronation taking place as scheduled: 'there is a certain vague grouping of cases on the basis of intuition or judgement' (p. 250). LeRoy and Singell (1987) argue that Knight's work is 'properly read as an analysis of the consequences of the fact that entrepreneurship is uninsurable for economic institutions and economic theory. Its purpose is not to argue that in some situations the probabilistic calculus is inapplicable' (p. 401). There is some doubt as to the consistency of Knight's views.

4 Thus, as Lawson notes, he may not properly belong in the matrix cell indicated.

5 Arrow (1984) also discusses the question of weight of the argument: 'Weight is not necessarily related to the dispersion of a distribution ... *a posteriori* distribution of a numerical distribution may have a larger standard deviation than *a priori*, though the former must certainly have a greater weight. [But] increases in weight and decreases in variance generally accompany each other' (p. 18).

6 Shackle (1969) makes this point well in his critique of the marginal efficiency of capital being predicated on a view of the reaction of other entrepreneurs: 'In requiring him [the entrepreneur] to "have regard" to the intentions of others, we are asking the impossible ... Each enterpriser can without inconsistency or absurdity be deemed to arrive at a personal marginal efficiency of capital. But this will be achieved by applying the private interpretative frame of his own experience to a body of evidence which is fragmentary and insubstantial even in regard to the present' (pp. 44–5). One example of this interdependence concerns the prediction of relative prices which depend on the actions of other investors (Harcourt 1972, p. 59).

7 There is nothing very surprising in all this. The students of economic methodology have always insisted that economics is necessarily based on parables: 'Irrespective of what they preach, economists actually behave in a way that is not inconsistent with that of Stewart's analytical school ... [which] has a strong resemblance to "storytelling" ' (Skouras 1982, pp. 116, 124). The parables abstract from

risk and uncertainty. The difference between normal and abnormal times is not that risk calculus can be used in the former, but rather that incrementalism works.

8 Reliability ratios are not in general known to the agent. But experience allows a person to develop an alertness to potential information about whether to choose a particular action, while simultaneously blocking alertness to other potential stimuli (Heiner 1983, p. 565).

9 Keynes too believed in the importance of convention as a determinant of behaviour, particularly at periods of heightened uncertainty when investors are held to fall back on extrapolation from the recent past and reliance on the view of others. But Keynes' arguments here are more instinctively right than rigorously argued. At times he explains convention by referring to the 'judgement of the rest of the world which is perhaps better informed' (1973, vol. XIV, p. 114); elsewhere, particularly in *The General Theory*, he presents it as a means of limiting losses; while in subsequent writings he explains the importance of convention in psychological terms as a barrier to incapacitating anxieties (Winslow 1989, p. 1180).

10 One puzzle in all this is how agents assess their C–D gaps if *ex hypothesi* probabilities cannot be accurately gauged. Heiner's (1986) argument is that agents develop an awareness of reliability over time, and thus 'Even though many situations . . . may be historically unique, we may still be able to classify them as favourable or unfavourable for selecting a particular action' (p. 67). It is worth noting that not all agents will react similarly. It depends on the individual assessment of competence in relation to difficulty – and of course on the assessment of losses and gains, which themselves are functions of attitudes towards risk. In a competitive game it is quite possible that increased complexity will favour a high-risk strategy for competent players.

11 It is sometimes argued also that uncertainty results in reduced turnover in financial markets. One city economist noted in reference to the Gulf crisis in August 1990: 'It is almost impossible to make rational investment decisions on the basis of what is happening so . . . don't do anything . . . the first decision you make is likely to be the wrong one' (*Financial Times*, 12 August 1990, p. III).

12 There are, in fact, two more complex considerations here. The first is that some agents may find L and G affected by uncertainty, e.g. where the advantage of pre-emption in (5.1) is increased for some agents. This introduces the possibility of apparently perverse reactions for some agents in keeping with the diversity noted earlier. A second consideration is that Heiner's reliability condition is

defined for a particular action, e.g. investing in fixed capital, but the reliability condition for the action complement (not investing) may imply different behaviour. We do not explore these complications here; the latter point is explained in Driver (1992).

13 The use of forecast error as a measure of uncertainty also depends on the properties of the forecast error and the period over which the averaging occurs. For example, an optimist may have a low forecast error in a run of good years. But reliability contains information on perceived accuracy in good and bad years.

14 Both these statements assume that the relative values of loss and gain are not too dissimilar.

15 For one thing, reliability itself is virtually unmeasurable, requiring knowledge of the joint distribution of perception and outcomes.

16 Mascaro and Meltzer (1983) argue for the use of (time series) variability of errors of stationary variables such as growth rates of output. One of the justifications offered for this approach is that 'high variability of the unanticipated growth rate increases the difficulty of detecting promptly any change in the growth rate' (p. 491). This reasoning is interesting, but somewhat limited. Much period-specific information has a bearing on how easy it is to predict the future; simply selecting variance of past error as a proxy for uncertainty seems incomplete. Uncertainty can exist even with zero forecast errors.

17 The index of dispersion used in this book is the standard deviation of growth rates. There are arguments for using a more complex measure which takes into account that the mean of the distribution is not necessarily the appropriate estimator about which to consider the dispersion. Thomas Mayer (1989) refers to an alternative coefficient of divergence which is analogous to the coefficient of variation but expresses the sum of the absolute value of pairwise differences over the sum of the estimates. In practice the two measures seem highly correlated.

18 It is important also to note that the convention implied by the reliability condition is a convention of action. It is not the case that beliefs are forced into a conventional mould; rather, agents are aware of the underlying complexity. It is possible that, as uncertainty rises, agents will cluster around some convention, not only in their actions but also in their forecasts. Interactive forecasting might also rise in such circumstances (Zarnowitz and Lambros 1987). We postpone until the following, empirical, chapter the difficult question of whether such phenomena - as might occur at very high levels of uncertainty - will reduce dispersion and so make our chosen indicator perform perversely.

19 This contrasts with an alternative view which argues that greater unpredictability leads agents to redouble their efforts to learn from information, given the increased value of learning.

20 There may also be variety induced by different attitudes towards prospective gains and losses from using information.

21 This conclusion would not appear to follow from the subjectivist view or variants on models of subjective probability such as Shackle (1969). The latter theory conceptualizes uncertainty as based on potential surprise at any given outcome (gain or loss). Shackle constructs a bivariate function (of the outcome and the potential surprise) which measures the power of the information to arrest the attention of the decision maker; the function increases with the absolute value of the gain or loss and the level of the associated surprise. The information can then be summarized – using a trade-off between surprise and outcome – as two (focal) points which represent the gain or loss that initially commands the attention of the decision maker (see also Ford 1983). It does not appear possible, however, to derive a measure of objective or 'social' uncertainty from this concept.

22 The standard deviation was constructed by assuming a uniform distribution across the range.

23 Surprisingly, the authors find that when a different source (the Livingstone survey) is used for dispersion estimates, the correlation between this dispersion and individual risk is much higher than before and significant at 1 per cent or less (p. 613).

24 Lawson (1987) points to the different positions of agents in terms of access to knowledge, which supports diversity. Knowledge has an absolute and a relative aspect, i.e. it can be rationally based but at the same time is true only relative to its context: 'Within relatively localized or similar contexts there should be greater varia-tion in such beliefs ... where the inhabitants partake in a wider range of occupations/social practices' (p. 969).

25 It is possible, however, that the first indicator of increased environ-mental complexity may often be a rise in average absolute forecast error. See the estimated equations for dispersion in the next chapter.

6

Dispersion as a Measure of Uncertainty

6.1 INTRODUCTION

There is little consensus in the literature over the measurement of risk and uncertainty in applied work. Sometimes the measure used is simply the variance across time of some economic variable such as the exchange rate (Gosling 1986). More often the variance of forecast error is used (Mascaro and Meltzer 1983; Wadhwani 1987).[1] The previous chapter has proposed dispersion as a measure of uncertainty to be used in the empirical estimation of investment relationships in later chapters. This chapter seeks to further defend the choice of this measure by showing that it responds plausibly to the forces that might reasonably be argued to affect uncertainty.

Section 6.2 discusses in general terms the origin of dispersion, i.e. the question of why and how economic forecasts differ. Section 6.3 outlines the determinants of dispersion; a formal version of this is set out in section 6.4. Possible bias in the dispersion measure as a proxy for uncertainty is discussed in section 6.5. The specification and estimation of dispersion are carried out in section 6.6. The specification is extended to include other variables in section 6.7, and the results of this are presented in section 6.8.

6.2 DIFFERENCES BETWEEN ECONOMIC MODEL FORECASTS

Serious forecasting is generally carried out on large multi-equation economic models, such as (in the UK) those of the National

Institute for Economic and Social Research (NIESR), the London Business School (LBS) and the Treasury (HMT). Many City forecasting teams will have access to versions of one or more of these models, though some will in the past have been content with simpler forecasting procedures.

Forecasts will differ partly because of the nature of the assumptions on which the models depend. For instance, there may be differences as to which variables are exogenous. There will also be differences between the models in the assumed response of some variables to changes in others. For example, different models will show different responses of wages or prices to demand conditions.

Modellers will often develop a feel for the way that the economy is reacting to a particular set of events. This intuition may well be out of line with the mechanistic forecast generated by the model concerned. In such circumstances, the forecaster may simply override the model forecast using judgement. Work done for the Bank of England suggests that these judgemental adjustments can be very large indeed, as table 6.1 makes clear. Although the period studied may well be somewhat unusual, the figures are instructive. The fact that judgement enters so heavily into the forecasts

TABLE 6.1 An example of the role of judgement in Economic Forecasts, 1981-2

		GDP growth (%)	Price inflation (%)
NIESR[a]	Main forecast	0.6	9.3
	Mechanistic	1.4	6.8
	Judgement	−0.8	2.5
LBS[b]	Main forecast	1.7	10.6
	Mechanistic	1.3	17.7
	Judgement	0.4	−7.1
HMT[c]	Main forecast	0.6	14.7
	Mechanistic	−2.4	13.9
	Judgement	3.0	0.8

[a] National Institute for Economic and Social Research, London.
[b] London Business School.
[c] *Economist* Intelligence Unit forecasts, using the UK Treasury model.
Source: Artis (1982)

suggests that dispersion will reflect subjective aspects of uncertainty which will be unlikely to be fully captured by more mechanistic proxy measures such as volatility.

We next turn our attention to modelling dispersion. This is done so as to understand the process causing the change in dispersion over time and as a check on the plausibility of the use of dispersion to measure uncertainty.

6.3   UNDERSTANDING DISPERSION

This section gives an intuitive preview of the theory in section 6.4, which derives measures that might have a bearing on forecast dispersion. For the non-technical reader it is sufficient to note that these measures include time volatility of the variable in question (i.e. growth or inflation volatility); the difference between current and lagged levels of the variable; past forecast errors; and measures of the gap between target and actual values.

The intuitive reasons for using these measures are as follows. Volatility should affect dispersion mainly through its corrupting effect on information quality. This causes the judgement or intuitive factor in forecasting to be given greater weight. The difference between current and lagged values is also a kind of volatility measure and represents the scope for differences in views when adaptive forecasting is a feature. Past forecast error will contribute to dispersion because forecasts may attempt to allow in varying degrees for previous forecast errors. Finally, a differential belief in a policy target set by government could justify the use of a target gap variable – representing the size of any policy adjustment. One such variable, defined in respect of the money supply during the Medium-Term Financial Strategy of the early and mid 1980s, will be shown to be particularly important.

Figure 6.1 attempts to show some of the forces acting on dispersion in flow-chart form. Not all of the variables shown are measurable and the model is only schematic; the formal model in the next section is more parsimonious in terms of the linkages admitted.

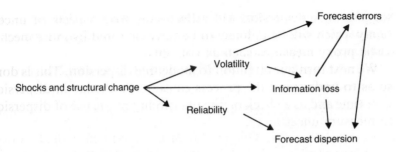

FIGURE 6.1   The structure of uncertainty

6.4   A THEORETICAL MODEL OF FORECAST DISPERSION

The model discussed in this section aims to explain the dispersion of forecasts across forecasting teams.[2] The variable whose dispersion is modelled at time t is P, which can stand for any endogenous variable forecast by a number of teams. It is assumed that the published (main) forecast is based partly on judgement, partly on mechanistic forecasting.[3]

Write the judgemental forecast of team i at time t as $\hat{P}_{i,t}^J$. Then assume

$$\hat{P}_{i,t}^J = \bar{P}_t^J + u_{i,t} \qquad (6.1)$$

where $\bar{P}_t^J$ is the mean judgemental forecast across teams, and $u_{i,t} \sim N(0, \rho_t^2)$ is a disturbance term reflecting differences of say optimism and pessimism.

The mechanistic forecast $\hat{P}_{i,t}^M$ can be model specific. If rational expectations are assumed,

$$\hat{P}_{i,t}^M = P_t + v_{i,t}, \quad v_{i,t} \sim N(0, \sigma_t^2) \qquad (6.2)$$

We assume that adaptive and rational expectations both operate:

$$\hat{P}_{i,t}^M = \begin{cases} P_{t-1} + \beta(P_{t-1} - \hat{P}_{i,t-1}^M) & \text{with probability } a \\ P_t + v_{i,t} & \text{with probability } 1-a \end{cases} \qquad (6.3)$$

We simplify the model by assuming that $a_i \equiv a$, i.e. that the structures of all models are similar and that models simply give different realizations of the same stochastic process.

Since the outcome set of $\hat{P}_{i,t}^M$ is binomial, its variance can be calculated as[4]

$$\phi_t^2 = [a(1 - a)(\Delta P_t + \beta e_{t-1})^2 + (1 - a)\sigma_t^2] \tag{6.4}$$

where $e_t = (P_t - \hat{P}_t)$. This may then be combined with the prior or judgemental variance term to give a variance for $\hat{P}_t$ of ω_t^2. Specifically, using the approach in Lindley (1965, p. 2) and Hogg and Craig (1971, p. 210), we have

$$\omega_t^2 = \rho_t^2 \phi_t^2 / (\rho_t^2 + \phi_t^2) \tag{6.5}$$

This estimate of uncertainty combines the sample and the prior variances; the combination is the inverse of the sum of the inverse variances. As either variance tends to infinity its influence on the combined measure vanishes, as information from this source would arguably be ignored by a rational assessor. If the prior distribution is uniform and log uniform in the mean and standard deviation, the judgemental forecast will be considered to be of little use. In this case its variance will not enter (6.5), which will instead simply be ϕ^2 (Phillips 1975).

Substituting (6.4) in (6.5) and linearizing, we get an expression for S_t, the standard deviation corresponding to ω_t^2:

$$S_t = f(\rho_t^2, \Delta P_t, e_{t-1}, \sigma_t^2) \tag{6.6}$$

A slightly different model can be generated if instead of the rational expectations term in (6.3) we substitute a policy target T. Assuming $\beta = 0$, we would then have an amended version of (6.6):

$$S_t = f(\rho_t^2, (T - P)_t, \sigma_t^2) \tag{6.7}$$

We have observations on the combined judgemental/mechanistic forecasts which can be used to generate values of S_t. We can also generate the data for each of the terms on the right hand side of (6.6) and (6.7), with the exception of ρ_t^2 which is unobserved.

6.5 CROSS-SECTION DISPERSION AND UNCERTAINTY: SOME QUESTIONS

In chapter 5 we have argued the merits of cross-section variation in expectations as an indicator of uncertainty. But it is necessary to introduce some qualifications to the claim of subjective variation to be a weather-vane for uncertainty. Firstly, it may well be the case that agents' expectations incorporate the asymmetric costs of being right or wrong or the asymmetric ease of adjustment in either direction. This case is argued in Aiginger (1987) for the slightly different case of industrial respondents to business surveys. He interprets such reported expectations as plans rather than statistical expectations in the usual sense. This is thought to explain why reported expectations consistently underpredict actual outcomes. This thinking can be extended by analogy to the case of professional forecasting teams. The cost penalties here may not be asymmetric, but there may be a cost attached to being far out of line with the median forecast. One recalls Keynes' dictum about the banker who preferred to be totally wrong in common with his peers than to chance being right in isolation.[5]

There are other criticisms of the use of variability as an indicator of uncertainty. One of these concerns the possibility that forecasts tend to cluster around some conventional norm when uncertainty is particularly high, for instance when the information required to make an informed judgement is lacking. In other words, does the dispersion across forecasts show a tendency to decrease at very high levels of uncertainty?

There is no entirely satisfactory way of investigating this question. What is at issue is whether the proposed measuring-rod of uncertainty – cross-section dispersion – is itself invariant with respect to uncertainty. Without an independent indicator of uncertainty, this question cannot be properly addressed. Zarnowitz and Lambros (1987) threw some light on this issue using survey responses on point forecasts and on individual probability distributions. Although they found a correspondence between the dispersion of point estimates and the dispersion of the predictive probability distributions, this correspondence was far from exact. One reason suggested was that 'it is precisely when uncertainty is high that people will have strong incentives to reduce the risk of making eccentric errors and will invest more resources in interactive prediction ... To the extent that this is true, it would tend to make the individual expectations (point forecasts) more closely bunched at such times' (p. 607). This reasoning runs somewhat counter to the Heiner view (discussed in chapter 5) that information is refused at times of greater complexity.[6] But even if it is not the case that agents search for more information as uncertainty rises, they might nevertheless increase interaction by exchange of views. This might result in increased consensus – the phenomenon we have called clustering.

In spite of the impossibility of rigour, owing to the lack of an independent objective measure of uncertainty, it is possible to test for clustering in a pragmatic way. The first maintained hypothesis is that no clustering exists. This is the focus of the test. The second maintained hypothesis is that we know the determinants of true uncertainty. This cannot be tested, as true uncertainty is unmeasurable. However, given this second hypothesis, it would be possible to detect clustering if the dispersion narrowed as the determinants of uncertainty took on values corresponding to high uncertainty. Put differently, dispersion measures uncertainty with error. If clustering occurs, the regression residuals will exhibit heteroscedasticity unless the regression also contains terms that proxy clustering.[7]

6.6   ESTIMATION AND RESULTS

The aim of the exercise reported here is to model dispersion and to understand its determinants, taking into account the possibility of clustering. The regressions reported in this section use as dependent variable the dispersion of forecasts. To be precise, it is the standard deviation across forecasting teams of the constructed one-year-ahead forecasts each quarter, based on the compilation of forecasts from up to twelve teams reported in the *Investors Chronicle* journal since 1976.[8] Some of these are City forecasts and some are academic ones. However, given the large judgemental element in forecasting noted earlier, all forecasts can be considered as comparable. Appendix 6.1 shows how the raw data can be transformed to yield quarterly estimates of year-ahead forecasts.[9]

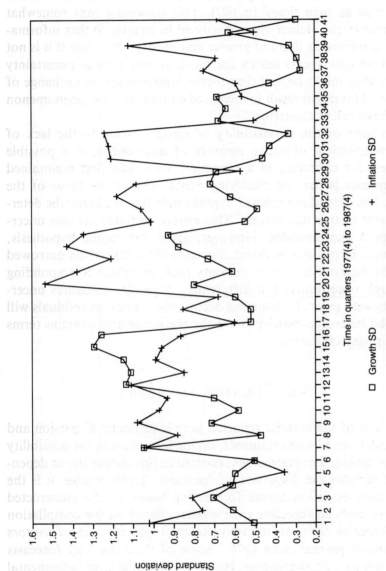

FIGURE 6.2 Dispersion indices

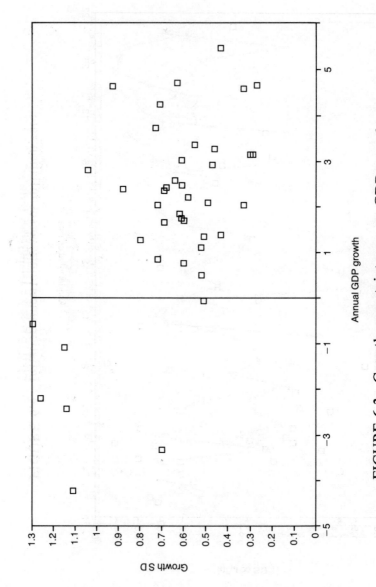

FIGURE 6.3　Growth uncertainty versus GDP growth

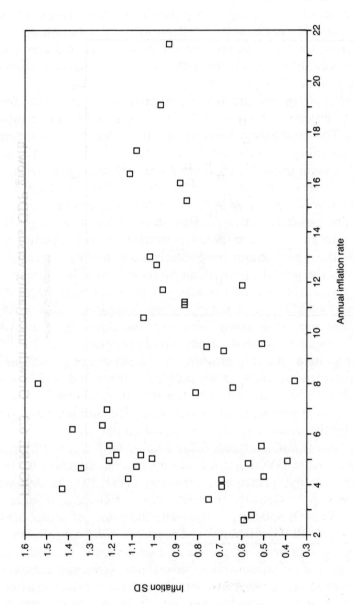

FIGURE 6.4   Inflation uncertainty versus inflation rate

A time plot of the dispersion indices formed by taking the cross-section standard deviation of the constructed forecasts is shown in figure 6.2. Both series have their peaks in the early 1980s. Plots of growth uncertainty against GDP growth and inflation uncertainty against the inflation rate are shown in figures 6.3 and 6.4. The main point of interest is the occurrence of high growth uncertainty at periods of negative growth.

A number of regressions are reported in this section for the subjective dispersion both of inflation forecasts and of growth forecasts. The explanatory variables are the forecast error, target gap and volatility measures (including first difference) suggested by the discussion in sections 6.3 and 6.4. Forecast error is defined as the sum over the previous four quarters of the absolute value of forecast errors, calculated as mean forecast minus revised actual value.[10] The gap between target and actual values is expected to be most relevant for the inflation regression, where government targets for the money supply were closely monitored by forecasters at least over the period of the Medium-Term Financial Strategy.[11] Volatility was measured in a number of different ways, most of which lead to highly correlated measures. A common set of volatility indices was constructed from these measures by means of principal component analysis, as discussed in appendix 6.2. Finally we have also used volatility measures of the *pattern* of growth and inflation, which we refer to as stability indices and which are defined later. The detailed results are shown in table 6.2, where the figures in parentheses are *t*-statistics. The sample sizes are dictated by the availability of the dispersion data.

The *growth equations* (table 6.2a) employ both a conventional volatility measure GVOL4 (four-quarter moving standard deviation) and the first principal component GVOLPC, as derived in appendix 6.2. Growth forecast error FEG (lagged once), along with growth volatility – especially the principal component measure – are all significant. The variable GSTAB measures stability in components of growth, i.e. the extent to which the quarterly growths in consumption, investment, government expenditure and exports are correlated with those in the previous quarter. As expected, greater stability appears to lower the dispersion. No significance could be found for the rate of change of the growth variable. The inclusion of the forecast error for inflation in the

TABLE 6.2 Forecast dispersion regression results: absolute *t*-statistics in parentheses

(a) Output growth SDGF, 1978(4) to 1987(4)

Variable	Equation				
	1	*2*	*3*	*4*	*5*
Constant	0.16	0.44	0.35	0.35	0.35
	(1.25)	(4.95)	(3.80)	(3.19)	(3.94)
FEG(−1)	0.23	0.16	0.16	0.14	0.14
	(3.80)	(2.87)	(3.00)	(2.60)	(2.73)
GVOL4	0.13				
	(1.88)				
GVOLPC		0.14	0.11	0.10	0.10
		(3.99)	(2.30)	(2.21)	(2.32)
FEI(−1)			0.04	0.04	0.04
			(1.65)	(1.92)	(1.96)
GSTAB(−1)			−0.10	−0.11	−0.11
			(2.20)	(2. 39)	(2.49)
DG				0.03	0.03
				(1.54)	(1.58)
ADG				0.00	
				(0.04)	
R^2	0.35	0.51	0.61	0.64	0.64
$\bar{R}^2$	0.31	0.48	0.57	0.57	0.59
DW	1.27	1.50	1.61	1.61	1.62
F	9.11	17.69	12.77	9.02	11.19
	(2,34)	(2,34)	(4,32)	(6,30)	(5,31)
SC: $\chi^2(4)$	6.72	3.52	4.72	5.25	4.93
FF: $\chi^2(1)$	4.45	1.79	0.01	0.41	0.36
N: $\chi^2(2)$	1.43	0.74	1.28	1.07	1.07
H: $\chi^2(1)$	4.85	0.45	1.22	1.52	1.54

(b) Inflation SDIF, 1978(4) to 1987 (2)

Variable	Equation			
	1	2	3	4
Constant	0.66	0.22	0.22	0.00
	(5.10)	(1.45)	(1.38)	(0.01)
FEG(-1)	0.17	0.37	0.38	0.40
	(1.94)	(5.05)	(4.54)	(5.27)
FEI(-1)	0.00	0.03	0.03	0.05
	(0.01)	(1.12)	(1.11)	(1.83)
IVOL4	0.01			
	(0.18)			
IVOLPC(1)			-0.02	
			(0.22)	
ISTAB(-1)		-0.16	-0.16	-0.18
		(2.25)	(2.21)	(2.57)
TGAP		0.17	0.16	0.22
		(4.22)	(2.79)	(4.65)
TGAPS		-0.02	-0.02	-0.02
		(5.00)	(3.60)	(5.43)
DI				0.04
				(1.70)
ADI				0.04
				(1.05)
R^2	0.14	0.56	0.56	0.61
$\bar{R}^2$	0.06	0.49	0.47	0.51
DW	1.03	1.78	1.78	2.21
F	1.75	7.42	5.99	6.12
	(3,31)	(5,29)	(6,28)	(7,27)
SC: $\chi^2(4)$	7.55	2.93	3.13	3.48
FF: $\chi^2(1)$	0.23	0.31	0.36	0.03
N: $\chi^2(2)$	1.73	0.72	0.85	0.22
H: $\chi^2(1)$	1.46	0.51	0.37	0.21

Table 6.2 continued

Variables

SDGF	output growth uncertainty: SD across twelve forecasting teams of growth rate in next twelve months
SDIF	inflation uncertainty: SD across twelve forecasting teams of inflation rate in next twelve months
FEG	sum over previous four quarters of absolute value of mean forecast error of output growth
GVOL4	four-quarter moving standard deviation of output growth
GVOLPC	first principal component of measures of growth volatility (see appendix 6.2)
FEI	analogous to FEG for inflation rate
GSTAB	correlation coefficient between growth rates at successive periods of components of output growth
DG	first difference of output growth rate
ADG	absolute value of DG
IVOL4	analogous to GVOL4 for inflation rate
IVOLPC	analogous to GVOLPC for inflation rate (see appendix 6.2)
ISTAB	analogous to GSTAB for inflation rate
TGAP	difference between current target for money supply and previous out-turn
TGAPS	square of TGAP
DI	first difference of inflation rate
ADI	absolute value of DI

Diagnostics

DW	Durbin-Watson statistic
SC	Lagrange multiplier test for fourth-order serial correlation
FF	Ramsey RESET test using squared fitted values
N	Jarque-Bera test for normality of residuals
H	heteroscedasticity test using regression of squared residuals on squared fitted values

Note: sample periods dictated by data availability.

growth equation is not strongly supported. The diagnostics are generally acceptable. The F form of the serial correlation test is more suitable for small samples, and this is generally passed. There is no support for entering a lagged dependent variable, suggesting that all the dynamics are contained in the levels equation.[12]

In the *inflation equations* (table 6.2b) the lagged dependent variable was also insignificant. In these regressions, dispersion is positively affected by forecast error FEI but not by volatility measures, defined analogously to the growth case. Furthermore the inflation dispersion appears to be influenced during the period of the Medium-Term Financial Strategy by a variable TGAP, which measures the gap between current year target for money supply and the out-turn in the previous year, i.e. it measures the ambitiousness of the target. The larger this gap the greater the dispersion, except that this relation appears to reverse itself at high levels of TGAP, as shown by the negative squared term. This indicates that an ambitiously stringent target causes forecasts to converge, as it indicates the seriousness of the government's message.[13] Inflation dispersion is influenced not only by its own forecast error but also by that of growth (FEG). Indeed the influence of the latter is even more significant than that of the former in the best equations. It has already been noted that this cross-effect is not strongly supported in the growth equations. This contrast is, perhaps, not surprising. If growth turns out differently from expected this should have an immediate effect on inflation expectations. But the effect of inflation forecast error on growth would be expected to be more indirect, mediated, for instance, by government policies as well as the action of firms. The stability measure in the inflation equations is defined as the correlation of some of its chief components: change in interest rate, growth in unit labour costs, and growth in raw material prices between the current and the previous quarter. Once again, this shows up as significantly lowering the dispersion. Finally, the influence of the rate of change of inflation has been found to be significant for both the absolute and the signed changes ADI and DI respectively. These were entered separately to capture any asymmetric effect of upward or downward changes. The diagnostics for these equations are all highly satisfactory.

What conclusions can be drawn from these regressions? Firstly, the hypothesized determinants of dispersion have largely been confirmed. The structure of the two equations for growth and inflation is quite similar, though volatility is replaced by the policy target variable in the inflation case. It is not surprising that the dispersion of a variable so heavily targeted by government is more related to forward-looking volatility, of which TGAP is a measure, than to the backward-looking measures relevant for growth.

Even in the best cases, however, there is still substantial variation. Subjective uncertainty as measured by cross-section variation, and environmental complexity as measured by forecast error, volatility etc., are evidently related, but by no means perfectly. This is not surprising as no attempt has so far been made to model the extent of the judgemental factors in amplifying the dispersion. Indeed it is somewhat surprising that the diagnostics on the fitted equations are so good; the omission of important variables would have been expected to lead to autocorrelated or heteroscedastic error terms. It may be that the factors hypothesized as affecting mechanistic forecasts are exactly those that enter into judgemental forecasts.

In terms of the clustering hypothesis, only a limited effect could be observed. Squared terms on variables were sometimes oppositely signed when entered in conjunction with the reported terms, but they were not generally close to significance. On the other hand, ambitious policy targets seemed to cause clustering.

6.7 EXTRA EXPLANATORY VARIABLES

We now turn to a consideration of other variables that might offer additional explanatory power in explaining dispersion. Two dimensions are considered. Firstly, the hypothesis that volatility affects dispersion is generalized so that volatility is measured for a wider set of variables. Secondly, an attempt is made to construct a set of general risk or uncertainty measures. These two innovations are discussed below.

6.7.1 *Volatility indicators*

The first expanded set of variables referred to above is a broad set of volatility measures on different economic variables. There are seven of these:

XVI *Volatility of output growth* This is defined as a four-quarter moving standard deviation of annual growth of GDP.

XV2 *Volatility of inflation rate* This is defined as a four-quarter moving standard deviation.

XV3 *Volatility of London share prices* This is defined as the sum of a four-quarter absolute deviation from a four-quarter moving average constructed over current and previous quarters.

XV4 *Volatility of short-term interest rates* This is defined as a four-quarter moving standard deviation of quarterly rates.

XV5 *Volatility of long-term interest rates* This is defined as a four-quarter moving standard deviation of twenty-year rates.

XV6   *Volatility of the exchange rate*   This is defined as a four-quarter moving standard deviation of the sterling–dollar rate.

XV7   *Volatility of the CBI optimism index*   This is defined as a four-quarter standard deviation of the balance of ups over downs in question 1 of the *Industrial Trends Survey* of the Confederation of British Industry (CBI).

These seven measures are chosen on pragmatic grounds, but they can be defended as plausible indicators of uncertainty. Volatility of growth rates and inflation rates can be justified in so far as they make it more difficult to notice changes in trend in these variables. Share price volatility is a measure of the strength of the 'news' factor. A purist might argue that this is the only measure of volatility needed since others involve double counting, but we are mindful of the possibility of fads in financial markets (Nickell and Wadhwani 1987). The volatility here is not expressed as a standard deviation as the series is highly trended; rather a measure of deviation from trend is used.

Volatility of interest rates both long and short are worth considering in that they convey information on uncertainty in respect of cost, liquidity and demand. Working capital is generally financed out of short-term loans. Because of this, the short rate influences corporate liquidity. Consumer liquidity will be influenced similarly with implications for consumer expenditure growth. Finally, a small part of total investment will also be financed from longer-term loans, particularly in the small-firm sector.

Exchange rate volatility has often been argued to depress exports because of the uncertainty effect. The evidence for this is mixed (Gosling 1986) but it is clearly plausible that this aspect of uncertainty will influence growth if it has, or is thought to have, an effect on exports. The UK effective exchange rate is probably most relevant for export prospects, but we have chosen to measure the sterling–dollar cross-rate as this will also have a bearing on import costs, in particular commodities which are denominated in dollars.

The CBI optimism question does not focus on any particular economic variable but allows these to be weighed in the minds of the survey respondents. The weight attached by the respondents to variables such as growth or inflation may of course vary over time. The volatility of this series should provide a subjective indicator of overall uncertainty in respect of profitability.

The correlation matrix for each measure in the volatility set suggested that some reduction in the dimension of the data set was possible. Accordingly principal component analysis was again used to extract the common variance. As shown in table 6.3, the first four components accounted for 84 per cent of the variance. These components may loosely be interpreted as follows:

XVPC1   This captures volatility of long and short interest rates, optimism and inflation. These contrast with tranquil stock market conditions.
XVPC2   This is dominated by growth volatility.
XVPC3   This mainly reflects exchange rate volatility.
XVPC4   This is dominated by share price volatility.

6.7.2   General uncertainty measures

There is no single measure that adequately captures subjective uncertainty. Nevertheless, it is possible to identify some economic series that contain information on this. These exclude volatility measures. Four proxy measures are outlined as follows.

TABLE 6.3   Results of principal component analysis on volatility measures XV1 to XV7

| | Principal components | | | |
	1	*2*	*3*	*4*
XV1	0.06	0.93	0.20	0.04
XV2	0.69	0.35	−0.39	0.39
XV3	−0.64	−0.36	−0.09	0.53
XV4	0.83	−0.08	−0.17	0.28
XV5	0.76	−0.39	−0.25	−0.17
XV6	0.32	−0.17	0.83	0.34
XV7	0.68	−0.16	0.39	−0.22
Cumulative % of variance explained	39.0	57.9	74.1	84.2

U1 *Uncertainty over demand*   The CBI *Industrial Trends Survey* elicits information on the percentage of respondents whose investment is constrained because of 'uncertainty about demand' (question 16c). It is possible that this question conflates the notion of pessimism over demand with that of genuine uncertainty. Accordingly we have taken the residual from a regression of this variable on another variable indicating the strength of expected demand. This variable was in turn constructed using the Pesaran method of transformation on the up–down survey responses in respect of the volume of total new orders (question 7) of the CBI survey (Wren-Lewis 1985). It may be noted that this measure, in common with the others to follow, relates only to manufacturing, this being the concern of the particular survey used.

U2 *Term structure*   The term structure of interest rates – the difference between long and short rates – is sometimes thought to reflect a risk premium, and this explains its use here. On occasions, however, the yield curve is negative, reflecting expectations that rates will be lower in the future. As the long rate does not immediately adjust fully to movements in the short rate, the term structure as measured by three-month to long-term rates is often just a reflection of what is happening at the short end of the market, e.g. as governments influence the short rate for policy reasons. For this reason we concentrate attention on the term structure, defined as a twenty-year rate minus a five-year one (Mankiw 1986).

U3 *Long-term growth uncertainty*   The data on team forecasts in the *Investors Chronicle* give forecasts for the current year and the next year. It is possible to manipulate the data to get a measure of the dispersion of the differences between short-term and longer-term forecasts. Where these differences are highly variable between forecasters, this may be taken as an indicator of subjective uncertainty, given that formal models are unreliable for periods of more than a few quarters ahead. Put differently, the proposed measure is intended to capture the extent of judgemental rather than mechanistic forecasts.

U4 *Long-term inflation uncertainty*   This is constructed analogously to the previous item.

6.8 FURTHER MODEL RESULTS

The volatility principal components and the variables representing general risk were then entered in the dispersion data for growth and inflation, along with some of the earlier variables, to see if there was a significant increase in explanatory power. The results are shown in table 6.4.

For the *growth equations* (table 6.4a) it is clear that the volatility measures are correlated with dispersion. However, on their own they account for only a third of the total variation and exhibit severe misspecification. None of the general uncertainty measures except the term structure (U2) came close to significance; with the addition of this and other terms from table 6.2, the equation passed all specification tests.[14] The $\bar{R}^2$ was considerably higher than for the best equation in table 6.2.

For the *inflation equations* (table 6.4b) the volatility terms were, in common with the results of table 6.2, insignificant. The only general uncertainty measure that reached significance was the long-term inflation uncertainty term (U4). The addition of this to the best equation from table 6.2 raised the $\bar{R}^2$ considerably. There are no specification problems here.

6.9 OVERALL CONCLUSIONS

Measures of dispersion – the standard deviation across forecast teams – have been constructed for growth and inflation for the UK economy 1976–89. It has proved possible to explain up to three-quarters of the variation of dispersion. The first approach was to attempt to explain dispersion of growth and inflation by indicators pertaining only to these two variables – mainly forecast error and measures of volatility. This yielded results which accounted for only half the variation. The second approach was to cast the net wider and to include a number of plausible measures of general uncertainty as well as further indicators of economic volatility. The addition of these variables further raised the explanatory power of the equations. One feature that is apparent in both sets of results is the contrast between the growth and inflation equations. In particular, volatility measures seem to play little part

TABLE 6.4 Extended results for forecast dispersion: absolute
t-statistics in parentheses
(a) Output growth, SDGF, 1979(4) to 1987(3)

Variable	Equation 1	Equation 2	Equation 3
Constant	0.68	0.33	0.28
	(16.06)	(3.40)	(2.68)
XVPC1	0.09		
	(2.06)		
XVPC2	0.08		
	(1.88)		
XVPC3	0.06	0.06	0.05
	(1.38)	(1.72)	(1.48)
XVPC4	0.08	0.07	0.05
	(1.96)	(2.20)	(1.55)
FEG(-1)		0.14	0.10
		(2.37)	(1.60)
FEI(-1)		0.06	0.05
		(4.41)	(3.42)
GSTAB(-1)		-0.06	-0.06
		(1.60)	(1.59)
U2		0.12	0.14
		(1.48)	(1.64)
SDGF(-1)			0.20
			(1.36)
R^2	0.33	0.73	0.75
$\bar{R}^2$	0.23	0.67	0.68
DW	0.88	1.46	1.74
F	3.38	11.32	10.30
	(4,27)	(6,25)	(7,24)
SC: $\chi^2(4)$	14.14	12.28	10.48
FF: $\chi^2(1)$	2.98	3.56	1.98
N: $\chi^2(2)$	1.47	1.62	2.27
H: $\chi^2(1)$	5.70	0.82	0.37

(b) Inflation SDIF, 1979(4) to 1987(2)

Variable	Equation 1	Equation 2
Constant	0.95	0.01
	(17.56)	(0.03)
XVPC1	0.08	
	(1.54)	
XVPC2	0.02	
	(0.33)	
XVPC3	0.04	
	(0.78)	
XVPC4	0.00	
	(0.07)	
FEG(−1)		0.38
		(5.14)
FEI(−1)		0.04
		(1.27)
TGAP		0.20
		(3.00)
TGAPS		−0.02
		(3.63)
DI		0.07
		(1.92)
ADI		0.07
		(1.13)
ISTAB(−1)		−0.14
		(1.91)
U4		0.24
		(2.04)
R^2	0.10	0.70
$\bar{R}^2$	–	0.59
DW	1.17	2.21
F	0.77	6.29
	(4,27)	(8,22)

Table 6.4 continued

Variable	Equation 1	Equation 2	Equation 3
SC: $\chi^2(4)$	6.24	7.96	
FF: $\chi^2(1)$	0.70	0.44	
N: $\chi^2(2)$	2.32	1.78	
H: $\chi^2(1)$	2.36	0.69	

For definitions of main variables and diagnostics, see table 6.2.
For definitions of additional variables XVPC1 etc. and U1 etc., see section 6.7.

in the latter. The importance of targets in causing dispersion comes across clearly.

This chapter has shown that dispersion, considered as a proxy for uncertainty, responds plausibly to its determinants. The next step is to use the constructed series for growth and inflation dispersion as explanatory variables in investment equations. This exercise is reported in chapter 7.

APPENDIX 6.1: THE CONSTRUCTION OF THE YEAR-AHEAD FORECASTS

We describe here the derivation of year-on-year forecasts from those published in the *Investors Chronicle*. The latter are forecasts made, on average, in March, June and September of each year for the current calendar year and the next calendar year. Thus only the forecasts made in December are year-ahead forecasts. Accordingly we constructed these year-ahead forecasts, e.g. for March

$$F(m) = [(1 + y)(1 + w) - 1]$$

where y is the forecast growth for March to December and w is the forecast for December to the following March. Thus

$$F(m) = [(1 + f_c(m))/(1 + g(m))]$$
$$[1 + (f_n(m) - 2S(m))/4] - 1$$

where $f_c(m)$ is the forecast for the current year, made in March; $g(m)$ is the actual output growth to March from the beginning of the current year; and $f_n(m)$ is the forecast for the next year, made in March. $S(m)$ is the slope per quarter of a line joining the current and next year forecasts, e.g. for March this is $[f_n(m) - f_c(m)]/4$. Although generally small, this correction is needed to allow for cases where forecasters record big differences between the current and next years. In such cases we would not expect the differences to be fully reflected in the early quarters of the next year.

The remaining year-on-year forecasts are constructed analogously.

APPENDIX 6.2: MEASURES OF VOLATILITY: THE CONSTRUCTION OF GVOLPC AND IVOLPC

There is more than one way in which the volatility of a time series can be measured. The basic measure employed is a four-quarter standard deviation taken over previous and current periods – a moving standard deviation. However, if the series is non-stationary this measure loses its intuitive appeal. For example, with a linear trend the measure will increase even if all the observations are exactly on trend. Often it is the conditional volatility that is relevant when constructing an uncertainty measure for use in regression equations, i.e. variance conditional on the information set (Pagan and Ullah 1986). However, we have argued above that the unconditional volatility is also relevant where it affects the accuracy of information. A general formulation would allow both of these to influence dispersion.

The conditional volatility is already represented in one form as variation in the mean forecast error. Other forms are nevertheless plausible, depending on how volatility is measured. Accordingly a number of other measures were also calculated. One of these is the four-quarter moving standard deviation of first differences of the series, which will estimate the unpredictability of the series if it is a random walk. It may be shown that the variance of a first difference is related to the variance of the level. Specifically, $\text{var } U = 2 \text{ var } U (1 - \rho)$, where ρ is the first-order autocorrelation coefficient (Kendall 1973, p. 51). It would not therefore be surprising to find a linear relation between this measure of volatility and the previous one. A third measure took the standard deviation about a (four-quarter moving average) trend. This is a commonly used measure and may reflect subjective assessment of volatility. Pagan and Ullah (1986) are critical of it partly because a predictable series will not always be recorded with zero volatility according to this measure (p. 19). A fourth measure recorded the mean absolute deviation from a moving average. In general, it depends on the underlying distribution whether the mean deviation or the absolute deviation is superior (Kennedy 1985, p. 25). The fifth and sixth measures were repeats of the first and second measures except that they were calculated for a longer interval (ten quarters). Finally, a novel measure of volatility was constructed to express the 'salience' of variability in the data. This seventh measure was a weighted sum of any shocks in the last ten quarters, where a shock was deemed to have occurred if an observation was more than two standard deviations from its ten-quarter moving average; the weight in each case was taken as the distance from the current period to the shock. Thus if a shock occurs in a particular quarter it would gradually die away over ten periods, unless a further shock ensued. Only peaks in the observations which occur suddenly rather than build up slowly are likely to be recorded by this measure.

Most of these measures were highly correlated both for growth and for inflation. Indeed, the first principal component for growth GVOLPC accounted for 60 per cent of the variation. This was a set of positive weights on all measures; the contrast between the four-quarter and the ten-quarter measures was largely responsible for variation independent of this. For inflation, the first six measures were highly correlated and the first component IVOLPC(1) accounted for 70 per cent of the variation. The shock of 'salience' measure was independent of the others and dominated the second principal component IVOLPC(2), bringing the cumulative explained variance to 84 per cent. This contrast with the growth case arises because the growth shock of the early 1980s occurred suddenly enough to be recorded as a shock by the strict definition above. On the other hand, the rise in inflation at the turn of the decade was not severe enough in relation to the immediately preceding period to count as a shock. Indeed the only occurrence of an inflation shock in the 1980s was in 1986(3), when inflation uncertainty as measured by the volatility measure was low by historical standards. IVOLPC(2), which is more or less the same as the inflation shock series, did not seem important in any of the regressions attempted for the analysis in table 6.2.

NOTES

1 The variance of forecast error is identical to the sum of the variance about the mean forecast and the squared mean error. In chapter 5 we have argued for the use of the variance about the mean forecast alone on the grounds that uncertainty should not be equated with deficient foresight. Nevertheless, it was recognized that dispersion and forecast error might not be independent. Dispersion might be affected by past forecast error and might reflect the same forces that generate forecast error.

2 Batchelor and Orr (1987) present a model of dispersion across individuals; the dispersion is partly due to individuals observing behaviour in a single market. This is obviously a context different from that of our model, which involves team dispersion and where the teams study all markets.

3 In the US this has been done formally by the National Bureau for Economic Research. In the UK it may be done informally.

4 The proof is as follows. Omitting the i subscripts, the variance of $\hat{P}_t^M$ is given by the variance of the expression in (6.3). The expected value of this expression is

$$\bar{P}_t^M = a(P_{t-1}\,\beta e_{t-1}) + (1-a)P_t$$

where e is the term in parentheses in (6.3). Writing

$$\text{var } \hat{P}_t^M = \sum f(P_t^M - \bar{P}_t^M)^2$$

we have

f	$(\hat{P}_t^M - \bar{P}_t^M)$	$(\hat{P}_t^M - \bar{P}_t^M)^2$	$[f(\hat{P}_t^M - \bar{P}_t^M)^2]$
a	$(1-a)x$	$(1-a)^2 x^2$	$a(1-a)x$
$1-a$	$(-a)x + v_t$	$a^2 x^2 + v_t$	$(1-a)a^2 x^2 + (1-a)v_t^2$

Thus

$$\text{var } \hat{P}_t^M = (1-a)ax^2 + (1-a)\sigma_t^2$$

where $x = \beta e_{t-1} - \Delta$ and $\Delta = P_t - P_{t-1}$.

5 It is also plausible that team forecasts will be more consensual than individual ones, with extreme views being discounted before publication. It is possible to test this for a short sample of observations by comparing the dispersion (standard deviation) for year-ahead inflation obtained from two sources. The first is the Barclays Bank BASIX index across individual respondents, which involves a large sample. The second is the dispersion across forecasting teams constructed from data in the *Investors Chronicle* and described in more detail later in the chapter. The comparison showed a close relationship between the two series but no consensus factor.

6 But see Blanchard and Dornbusch (1983): 'For academics and forecasters . . . uncertainty acts as a spur to further research gathering and "differentiation" ' (p. 156).

7 Previous work in this area does not seem to have addressed this question. Batchelor (1985) regressed subjective dispersion on the level and volatility (time standard deviation) of inflation, without finding a significant role for volatility. Batchelor and Orr (1987) did find a significant role for volatility using a more sophisticated model and entering other variables, but the relationship was unstable for subperiods over the range 1962–74, with a break after 1973.

8 We are grateful to Ken Holden for making some earlier data available to us and for drawing our attention to the series.

9 The standard deviation across forecasting teams is our chosen measure of variation. There has been some discussion (e.g. Aiginger 1987) as to whether the standard deviation or the coefficient of variation is a more appropriate term. This links with the much researched question of whether inflation and inflation variability are causally linked. Driffill et al. (1989) argue that any such link is not causal.

10 The use of revised data is of course questionable. But it is not clear that any correct procedure exists for measuring perceived forecast error. Measurement of this depends on how agents come to a perception of true outcomes, whether by ascertaining published figures or in some other way.

11 We are grateful to Philip Arestis for making these data available from Arestis and Skuse (1989).

12 This contrasts with the results in Batchelor and Orr (1987).

13 Note that if TGAP, suitable scaled, were considered a proxy for $1 - a$ in (6.3), then the signs on the TGAP terms in table 6.2b would be as expected. In that case the variable target minus expected inflation, proxied by terms in the money supply, would also be expected to be

significant. Our attempts to estimate this were dogged by instability due to the multicollinearity in the various terms.

14 Although the χ^2 form of the autocorrelation test was failed, the F form was satisfactory.

7

Estimating the Effect of Uncertainty: Aggregate Investment

7.1 INTRODUCTION

This chapter is concerned with the estimation of uncertainty effects on investment. The study uses data for plant and machinery expenditure on UK manufacturing in the 1970s and 1980s. Section 7.2 interprets the uncertainty variables in a theoretical context. The hypotheses for the estimation are outlined in section 7.3. Functional forms are discussed in 7.4. Two specific estimation sets are reported in sections 7.5 and 7.6. The conclusions are noted in section 7.7.

The focus on manufacturing is not intended to imply a ranking in importance; that is a separate issue. However, studies of manufacturing investment are well documented and there is general agreement on broad specification.[1] This contrasts with the service sector where it has proved more difficult to find simple stable relationships. There are other reasons for narrowing the dependent variable to plant and machinery expenditure – the major component of manufacturing investment. Firstly, it makes sense to disaggregate by type of investment since the nature and economic purpose of the expenditure may differ between categories. Secondly, endogeneity problems occasioned by contemporaneous output terms are lessened when the investment variable is only a part of total investment. Thirdly, the lags are much shorter for plant and machinery and this allows us to conserve degrees of freedom. Finally, plant and machinery data are better predicted by managers (Lund et al. 1976, p. 60) and thus may serve as a better basis for control than new building, which is less predictable in expenditure and timing.

Nevertheless, one disadvantage of our focus is that substitution between categories of investment may not be adequately modelled. For example, a reasonable hypothesis is that uncertainty shortens payback and may therefore cause a switch from longer-lived projects such as new building to 'efficiency' investment involving plant and machinery. Were such a substitution effect to dominate, it would imply a positive relationship between uncertainty and plant and machinery investment.

7.2 THE UNCERTAINTY VARIABLES

The specifications developed are tested for the exclusion of variables measuring uncertainty, as proxied by the dispersion indicators suggested in chapter 6. Because of limitations in our data we are confined to studying the effects of output uncertainty and price uncertainty. To a certain extent these uncertainty measures may act as proxies for uncertainty over other variables such as interest rates or exchange rates, or even productivity. However, it is unlikely that our measures will capture forms of uncertainty specific to individual firms or industries. For example, the timing of government emission controls may be of concern to companies in the car industry, while uncertainty over agreements on world trade may feature in open sectors. Unlike the effects of many other economic variables, these effects do not cancel out in the aggregate but rather are cumulative. We are therefore only modelling a part – albeit an important part – of uncertainty facing decision makers.[2]

The theoretical role for our constructed measures of uncertainty must now be clarified. The models discussed in chapter 4 referred to different competitive regimes. Price uncertainty was seen as relevant for competitive price-taking firms, while demand uncertainty applied to firms operating under imperfect competition. However, the relationship between these concepts and our empirical measures of uncertainty is not transparent. In particular, the relationship between demand uncertainty and empirical measures of uncertainty in respect of output needs to be clarified.

A number of interpretations of the uncertainty measures are

TABLE 7.1   Possible states of uncertainty

	Uncertainty relates to:	
	demand curve	*demand and supply curve*
Equilibrium	A	C
Disequilibrium (price rigidity in response to demand)	B	D

possible, depending on whether we adopt an equilibrium or a disequilibrium framework. The interpretation also depends on whether uncertainty is perceived in respect of the aggregate demand or aggregate supply curves. Table 7.1 summarizes some possibilities according to whether or not equilibrium product markets obtain and also whether perceptions of uncertainty relate solely to demand curves or to a combination of demand and supply schedules. We do not consider the unlikely case of pure cost uncertainty where only the supply curve varies. In reading the table it should be noted that disequilibrium is used in the special sense that, while prices adjust to changes in cost, they do not respond to shifts in demand. This characterization of equilibrium is not the only one possible, but it appears to accord with observed practice (Domberger 1980).

Table 7.1 may be related to the supply and demand variation shown in figure 7.1. D_0 and S_0 refer respectively to the expected positions of the demand and supply curves in the product market. For the purpose of this exposition we use the term 'uncertainty' to refer to the conceived range of variation in the shifts of these curves (D_1 to D_2 and S_1 to S_2).

For case A of table 7.1, equilibrium positions will be traced out along a fixed supply curve S_0, giving revealed uncertainty in price and output, with the cross-section distribution of these variables being perfectly correlated. Price variation is in the range $\{P(D_1:S_0), P(D_2:S_0)\}$, and quantity variation is captured by the range read off from this using the S_0 supply schedule. Empirical data tend to reject the hypothesis of perfect correlation between uncertainty in price and output, so this case is unlikely to be general.

For case B, price uncertainty should be zero. Quantity uncertainty will be more severe than for case A since conceived output variation will be higher in the face of non-adjusting price. In figure 7.1 the range of conceived quantity variation is shown as the heavy horizontal line through $(S_0:D_0)$, representing the range $\{Q[D_1|P(D_0:S_0)], Q[D_2|P(D_0:S_0)]\}$. Empirical work tends to reject the notion of minimal price uncertainty, however measured, so again this case will not be general.

Case C will be similar to case A, if uncertain forces such as technology shift the conceived demand curves and supply curves simultaneously by a related amount; this will again translate into perfectly correlated ranges of variation for output and price. More generally, the correlation between price and output measures of uncertainty will depend on the extent of independence between shifts in the demand and supply curves. In general, it cannot be assumed that the range of conceived variation in output bears any simple relationship to demand curve variation (demand uncertainty). The relevance of this case cannot be judged by correlation analysis; it is necessary to assess whether the equilibrium model is realistic.

For case D, price uncertainty will reflect uncertainty in respect of the supply curve alone. The range of price variation will be $\{P(D_0:S_1), P(D_0:S_2)\}$. Quantity uncertainty will reflect uncertainty in respect of (shifts in) the demand curve as well as uncertainty over induced changes in demand implied by price variations. The range of quantity variation is given by the dashed range along the horizontal axis of figure 7.1, which may be expressed as $\{Q[D_1|P(D_0:S_1)], Q[D_2|P(D_0:S_2)]\}$.

Discrimination between the empirically admissible models C and D is important since the interpretation of uncertainty measures differs between them. For the equilibrium case C, both of the empirical uncertainty measures contain information on *both* price and demand uncertainty. For the disequilibrium case D, the empirical price measure contains information on price uncertainty only, while the empirical quantity measure contains information

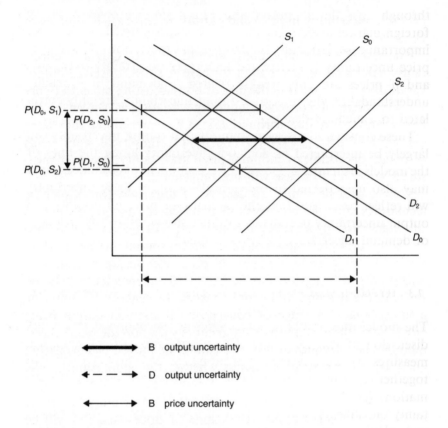

FIGURE 7.1   Supply and demand variation with reference to table 7.1

on both price and demand uncertainty. For the disequilibrium case, then, the effect of demand uncertainty can be isolated by considering the empirical quantity measure, conditioned on the price measure.

There is support for the disequilibrium case in the post-Keynesian literature on pricing and demand, reviewed in Sawyer (1985), Hay and Morris (1991) or Scherer (1980). Aiginger (1987) presents survey evidence to the effect that 'price plays the role as a comparatively fixed exogenous condition, predetermined through cost developments and long-term components or by foreign market leaders' (p. 156). This suggests that D is the most important case, especially for short-term expectations. If domestic price uncertainty is interpreted as largely uncertainty over costs and if prices are only weakly related to demand, it is readily understandable why price and output uncertainty are only correlated to a medium degree.[3]

These considerations seem to imply that output uncertainty can largely be interpreted as demand uncertainty along the lines of the models in chapter 4. However, a component of cost uncertainty may also be reflected in the output measure. Price uncertainty will reflect costs, and thus the joint use of price uncertainty and output uncertainty in statistical studies should allow the influence of demand uncertainty to be ascertained.[4]

7.3 HYPOTHESIZED EFFECT OF UNCERTAINTY ON INVESTMENT

The model interpretations of chapter 4, the bounded rationality discussion of chapter 5 and the interpretation of the empirical measures of uncertainty in section 7.2 can now be brought together to provide some general hypotheses for investment estimation. We expect a long-run depressing effect of demand uncertainty on capacity. The omission of uncertainty may be expected to lead to structural breaks in a regression equation for capital input. Finally, we note that our sample may include industries with different degrees of price flexibility and that the competitive models with price uncertainty alone imply an ambiguous effect of uncertainty on capital input (Aiginger 1987, pp. 44, 84).[5]

Will investment be revised permanently as a consequence of uncertainty, or will any effect be only transitory? The models of chapter 4 imply that a *permanent* change in uncertainty will have a permanent effect on investment and desired capital – unless of course some costless way of accommodating or hedging against the uncertainty is found. Similar arguments apply to the Heiner conventional response to uncertainty discussed in chapter 5. This suggests that capital input will reflect the level of uncertainty.

7.4 FUNCTIONAL FORMS: FORMULATING AN INVESTMENT EQUATION

The only models that will concern us here involve a putty-clay assumption, where capital–labour composition has to be decided *ex ante*. The irreversibility of investment is confirmed by patchy markets for second-hand capital goods; models involving the opposite assumption must be regarded as a special case. Irreversibility implies a putty-clay model unless there is considerable scope for reallocation of factors across technologies or product lines. This chapter follows a vintage approach to investment modelling, since production technology is generally fixed for machines already installed.

An investment equation can be derived by minimizing total production costs on all vintages subject to the output target. Given the target output level, decisions are made on the quantity to produce on existing vintages (the scrapping rule) and the capital intensity of new capacity. Cost minimization leads to an optimal or equilibrium investment equation which is log-linear in required new capacity YV and the relative price of factors of production c/w (King 1972).

Required new capacity YV is required output not produced on existing vintages – the latter being dependent on the (unknown) history of vintages. King (1972), Peterson (1976), Sarantis (1979) and Catinat et al. (1987) all take YV as a linear function of change in actual output Y. In our specification we have followed this, but we have made an attempt to correct for disequilibrium effects or echo effects by modifying the output change term by a variable scrapping rate $\hat{\delta}$.[6]

A second modification is made to the YV term to take into account the rate of capacity utilization. $Y(-1)$ will not necessarily be a good indicator of potential capacity at time $t-1$, and it is potential capacity that is important to the argument as this in turn determines required new capacity. One solution would be to convert $Y(-1)$ into potential capacity Y^* by dividing through by the capacity utilization $(Y/Y^*)(-1)$ or $u(-1)$. But to leave it like this would imply a rather odd situation in which investment was estimated assuming that all old capacity would be run at full capacity. Since it is rarely the case that full capacity is achieved throughout industry, the implication would be that new capacity was underused. It seems more sensible to argue that the old capacity will be run at the current rate of capacity in any period. Assuming that this current utilization u is estimated, along with output, when the investment is planned, the capacity at time t with no new investment is $[(u/u(-1))(1 - \hat{\delta})Y(-1)]$. Subtracting this from current output, we get a expression for YV.

In addition to the variables specified by King (1972), profitability may also be justified as a regressor, either because in expectational form it is a measure of Tobin's Q or, more esoterically, because it is a measure of the cost of non-supply arising from being unable to meet an uncertain demand (Malinvaud 1983). Alternatively it could proxy liquidity (Martin and O'Connor 1981) or expectations – 'animal spirits'.

As for the uncertainty variables, there is little in the way of robust or general theory to guide us in the choice of how uncertainty should be entered. One possibility would be to argue on practical grounds that uncertainty tends to raise the hurdle rate of return.[7] If this were so, we could formulate a composite cost of capital term to include uncertainty. However, much of the empirical evidence suggests that relative prices work on investment with a long lag, whereas we wish to test for the possibility of uncertainty affecting investment with a fairly short lag.

One further specification problem is that uncertainty may be expected to affect both optimal capacity and output. This raises a specification challenge because standard investment models determine optimal capital stock conditional on output, i.e. the equilibrium capital–output ratio.

Some theoretical models do imply a particular functional form for the uncertainty variable in investment equations. Since there are a great number of possible models, we describe below the one which seems to us most likely to be representative. Lambert and Mulkay (1987) use a specification for investment under demand uncertainty with endogenous output and fixed (certain) costs and price. The model assumes CES *ex ante* and Leontief *ex post* production functions along with multiplicative uncertainty and a log-normal distribution of demand. The implication – as might be expected of a model where the marginal cost of uncertainty features – is that investment depends on the interactive effect of uncertainty and profitability. Unless profitability is very high, demand uncertainty exerts a downward bias on the capital–labour ratio compared with the case of certain demand. The intuition behind the latter result is that capital, once installed, has to be fully supported, while labour input is assumed to be more flexible. Thus a negative influence of uncertainty on the equilibrium capital–output ratio may be inferred.

This model will inform the specification tests to follow. However, it cannot be regarded as a general model. Not only does it contain many untested assumptions but, crucially, it assumes risk neutrality for both the output and the capital input decision. This assumes that attitudes to risk are the same for output and capital input, which seems unlikely.[8]

We will, therefore, prefer to approach the data with a fairly open mind on the exact functional form in which uncertainty enters. Accordingly, we will allow the uncertainty variable to enter the equation on its own and with a lag to be freely determined.[9] Our prior beliefs are informed by the material in chapters 4 and 5, namely that uncertainty tends to depress and smooth the adjustment of capacity. Variation in uncertainty should therefore condition the adjustment path, and this can be modelled by complementary adjustment terms in uncertainty. We also expect to observe a long-run negative influence of demand uncertainty on the capital–output ratio.

The following two sections develop two different investment specifications – the first based on levels estimation and the second using the error correction approach. Data considerations constrain the estimation period – runs of quarterly data from 1978. This provides a respectable number of data points, but less historical variation than we would ideally like. Some tentative results will also be presented for a somewhat longer period using annual data. This annual study, reported in appendix 7.1, uses a slightly different methodology, but it is reported because of the longer timespan that it covers.

Data sources for the estimation are given in appendix 7.2.

Adopting the specification of King (1972), desired investment $I*$ is a log-linear function of required output YV, relative prices c/w and profitability π:[10]

$$\log I* = a + b \log YV - e \log(c/w) + f \log \pi \qquad (7.1)$$

A Koyck adjustment is often proposed for delivery and gestation lags (Catinat et al. 1987). Thus, adding a time parameter t,

$$\log I(t) = s \log I*(t) + (1 - s) \log I(t - 1) \qquad (7.2)$$

This represents a partial adjustment to the desired term.[11]

Equations (7.1) and (7.2) may be combined into an estimable equation:

$$\log I(t) = B_0 + (1 - s) \log[I(t - 1)] + B_1(L) \log[YV(t)] \\ + B_2(L) \log[(c/w)(t)] + B_3(L) \log[\pi(t)] \qquad (7.3)$$

where L is a lag operator. The term in $\log \pi$ can be interpreted as a determinant of 'desired' investment analogous to the relative price term. Alternatively, it is possible to interpret it, in first-difference form, as part of a variable-lag adjustment, where s is a linear function of change in profitability relative to the increase in investment required in the current period. Thus

$$s = s_0 + s_1[\Delta \log \pi / (\log I* - \log I(t - 1))] \qquad (7.4)$$

This is a cruder version of the formulation in Nickell (1978, p. 263), who criticizes the above on the grounds that s does not have an upper bound of unity. However, it has been extensively used, perhaps because of its tractability. After manipulation, it yields a coefficient on the lagged dependent variable of $1 - s_0$ and a coefficient on $\Delta \log \pi$ of s_1, with the rest of (7.3) unchanged. This interpretation of the profitability variable is likely to have some validity. Variable lags seem quite likely in practice if for no other reason than trade credit is a cyclical variable. Sarantis (1979) uses a cash flow variable rather than a profitability variable on the grounds that investment is constrained by liquidity. In practice, profitability and liquidity are likely to be highly correlated. However, profitability could be justified as a determinant of the lag length in that it alters the cost of adjustment occasioned by disruption to existing sales. Equation (7.3) is broadly similar to the form used by Catinat et al. (1987), though these authors also used a time trend. We tried to replicate the model of these authors and observed, as they did, that the equation was rather unstable when output and profitability were entered together.[12] Because of this, the equation reported in table 7.2 excludes profitability. The output growth dispersion term is included, but the inflation dispersion term was not close to significance and was omitted.

TABLE 7.2   Investment (log I) equation with uncertainty for UK manufacturing plant and machinery, 1978(4) to 1987(4)

Variable[a]	Coefficient	t-statistic
Constant	0.96	1.42
log $I(-1)$	0.70	6.40
log YV	0.19	0.83
log $YV(-1)$	0.11	0.45
log$(c/w)(-5)$	−0.03	−1.95
log $\sigma_g(-2)$	−0.08	−3.08

$R^2 = 0.94$, $\bar{R}^2 = 0.92$, DW = 1.65

SC: $F(4,24) = 0.76$
FF: $F(1,27) = 2.00$
N: $\chi^2(2) = 0.99$
H: $\chi^2(1) = 1.50$

[a] Three seasonal (quarterly) dummy variables were also included.

Variables:
I plant and machinery gross domestic fixed capital formation at constant prices
YV $Y - Y'(-1) + \hat{\delta}Y'(-1)$, where Y is index of manufacturing output at constant prices, $\hat{\delta}$ is constructed depreciation rate, and $Y'(-1)$ is potential output on old vintages assuming *current* capacity utilization
c/w relative price of capital and labour services
σ_g output growth uncertainty: SD across twelve forecasting teams of growth rate in next twelve months

Diagnostics
DW   Durbin-Watson statistic
SC   Lagrange multiplier test for fourth-order serial correlation
FF   Ramsey RESET test using squared fitted values
N   Jasque-Bera test for normality of residuals
H   heteroscedasticity test using regression of squared residuals on squared fitted values

The diagnostics in table 7.2 are all acceptable. The lack of significance for an output term is somewhat surprising. As they stand, the estimates imply a unitary elasticity of investment with respect to required output. There is a marked adverse effect of output growth uncertainty on investment, with a long-run static elasticity of about 0.24, nearly three times that for relative prices, where the effect is also less well determined.

7.6 ERROR CORRECTION APPROACH

We now turn to consider an alternative framework where the target and the dynamics are modelled simultaneously.[13] The dynamic specification is informed by Bean (1981), where investment orders are modelled in error correction form. Applying a delivery lag of n periods, this yields an equation for investment expenditure I:

$$\Delta_j \log I(t) = a + A(L) \Delta_j \log YV(t - n) + b[\log I(t) \\ - \log YV(t - n)] (-j) \tag{7.5}$$

where the lag structure and order of difference j are to be suggested by unrestricted estimation.

Feedback plays an important role in investment, with firms controlling their expenditure by cancellations and extensions to their previous orders (Nickell 1978, p. 290). This can be modelled by derivative (the change term), proportional (the error correction term) or integral (sums of error correction terms) control (Salmon 1982).[14] In the estimation reported in the following, it was found that the combination of a single derivative control term with a number of proportional terms or with integral control gave the most satisfactory results.[15] The specification is completed with the inclusion of lagged terms in relative price and profitability. The uncertainty variables are entered separately.

It remains to test for cointegration between the main variables, since the usual t test on the error correction form can be biased (Banerjee et al. 1986; see also Granger 1986). With nine lags, we found both $\log I$ and $\log YV$ to be integrated of order one, using the augmented Dickey and Fuller (1981) test (ADFT). The relevant t-statistics were 2.27 and 1.83 respectively, both below the critical value of 3.17, indicating that these variables are integrated of order one (Granger 1986).[16]

To test for cointegration, the ADFT was performed on the residuals of the cointegrating regression:

$$\log I(t) = a + h \log YV(t) + u(t) \tag{7.6}$$

The relevant t-statistic was 2.70, but rose to 3.86 when the insignificant fifth and sixth lags on the residuals were excluded. The Durbin-Watson statistic from (7.6) was 1.17 – above the 5 per cent critical upper limit for the null of non-cointegration (Sargan and Bhargava 1983). This test establishes that $\log I - h \log YV$ is stationary. The data supported a value of unity for h, and on this basis we felt justified in adopting the error correction specification used here.[17]

Inspection of the unrestricted estimates suggested the equation structure shown in table 7.3. The results are presented for three different equations: (1) a basic model with no uncertainty; (2) the same model with uncertainty terms; and (3) a model with integral control feedback on output and with uncertainty terms.[18]

The first equation in table 7.3 shows strong support for the accelerator model, modified by relative prices and profitability terms. The lag on the profitability and relative prices impact terms are longer than on output; this is in keeping with earlier results (Catinat et al. 1987). The lack of significance for a long-run profitability effect suggests that variation in profitability affects the timing but not the level of investment when required output is also present as a regressor. No specification problems are apparent from the diagnostics, though the Durbin-Watson statistic is somewhat low.[19] The restrictions implicit in the equation arising from the differencing procedure were found to be easily accepted with a value $F(9,23) = 0.58$.

The second equation shows a marked improvement (seven points) in $\bar{R}^2$ when the uncertainty terms are added. The t-values on both impact uncertainty effects are significant at the 5 per cent critical level. It may be noted that the coefficients on the change and lagged level of output uncertainty are almost identical, suggesting that it is only the current level that matters. The output uncertainty term exerts a significant long-run influence on investment. No long-run effect of inflation uncertainty is apparent.[20]

TABLE 7.3 Investment ($\Delta_4 \log I$) equations for UK manufacturing plant and machinery, (1978(4) to 1987(4): t-statistics in parentheses.

Variable	Equation 1	Equation 2	Equation 3
Constant	1.41 (5.31)	1.64 (7.64)	1.58 (7.27)
$\Delta_4 \log YV(-4)$	0.64 (1.79)	0.93 (2.84)	1.00 (3.03)
$\Delta_4 \log (c/w)(-8)$	−0.07 (4.53)	−0.04 (3.36)	−0.04 (3.45)
$\Delta_4 \log \pi (-8)$	0.18 (3.90)	0.17 (4.64)	0.16 (4.24)
$\Delta_4 \log \sigma_g$		−0.08 (3.87)	−0.08 (3.54)
$\Delta_4 \log \sigma_{\dot{P}}$		−0.05 (2.89)	−0.05 (2.69)
EC(YV)	−0.51 (5.20)	−0.61 (7.53)	−0.15 (7.22)
$\log (\sigma_g)(-4)$		−0.09 (2.70)	−0.07 (2.16)
R^2	0.86	0.92	0.91
$\bar{R}^2$	0.83	0.90	0.89
DW	1.53	2.28	2.14
SC	$F(4,26) = 0.89$	$F(4,21) = 1.47$	$F(4,25) = 1.41$
FF	$F(1,29) = 1.72$	$F(1,24) = 0.45$	$F(1,28) = 0.38$
$N{:}\chi^2(2)$	1.45	2.31	1.59
$H{:}\chi^2(1)$	0.14	0.01	0.06

Variables and diagnostics are as for table 7.2, with the addition of the following variables:
π profit rate in manufacturing
$\sigma_{\dot{P}}$ inflation uncertainty: SD across twelve forecasting teams of inflation rate in next twelve months
EC(YV)   error correction term: for equations 1 and 2, coefficient on sum of second-order Almon lag with no restrictions over lags 4 to 7 on [$\log I - \log YV (-1)$] $(t - i)$; for equation 3, integral control type, i.e. sum of terms in Almon lag in equation 2.

The short-run profitability term remains stable under the addition of the uncertainty terms and achieves increased significance. The impact term in relative prices remains significant with a reduced coefficient, while both the impact and long-run accelerator terms seem better determined.

The third equation shows the results with integral control on output. The parameters are largely unchanged, and the diagnostics are similarly satisfactory.

We have also tested for stability. Catinat et al. (1987) were unable to find a stable equation for UK manufacturing (all assets). Their moving regression estimates suggested a break in the early

TABLE 7.4   Test statistics for stability

Table 7.3 equation	Parameter stability	Variance equality	Predictive failure
1	$F(7,23) = 4.40$	$F(8,15) = 1.85$	$F(4,26) = 1.66$
2	$F(10,17) = 1.11$	$F(5,12) = 1.21$	$F(4,23) = 1.48$
3	$F(8,21) = 1.12$	$F(7,14) = 1.10$	$F(4,25) = 2.47$

See text for description of test statistics.

1980s, possibly during 1982. To test for this in our sample, we have split the period into roughly two halves: 1978(4) to 1982(2), and 1982(3) to 1987(4). We then carried out a number of stability tests between the samples for the equations in table 7.3.

The test statistics are shown in table 7.4. The parameter stability test is a Chow test which relies on a comparison of the unrestricted sum of squares from the two subsamples and the overall restricted sum of squares. The Chow test of parameter stability is really a composite test of equality of variance between samples and parameter stability. Accordingly, we also report a specific test for variance equality. This is the Goldfeld-Quandt test on the ratio of the residual variances. The predictive failure test, which can be interpreted as a general specification test, is a Chow test using the whole sample and the sample omitting the last four observations.

The parameter stability test is failed at the 5 per cent level for equation 1, but all the test statistics are satisfactory for the equations with uncertainty.

The long-run relationships implicit in equations 2 and 3 are similar, with a long-run elasticity for investment with respect to output uncertainty of about 0.15. This finding of a long-run role for output uncertainty is of great interest. It would be surprising indeed if there were no short-run effects for uncertainty, however measured, as firms may be expected to delay commitment for longer periods as uncertainty rises. The size of the uncertainty coefficient is moderate, though not negligible.[21] It is comparable with the long-run elasticity of investment to the standard deviation of expected demand (0.17) estimated by Artus and Muet (1990).

A graph of the actual and the fitted values from the integral

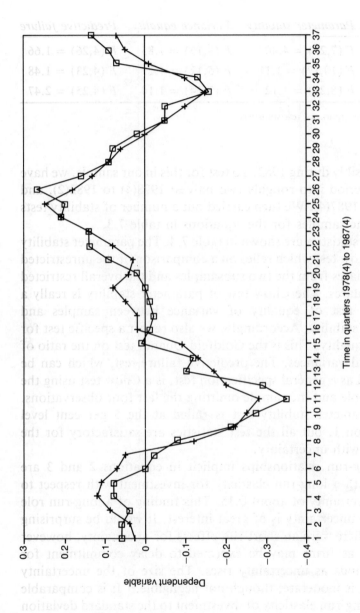

Time in quarters 1978(4) to 1987(4)

□ actual   + fitted

FIGURE 7.2 Investment without uncertainty

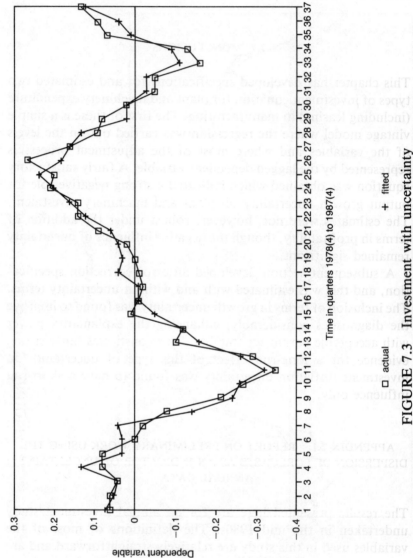

FIGURE 7.3 Investment with uncertainty

Time in quarters 1978(4) to 1987(4)

□ actual   + fitted

Dependent variable

control equation (equation 3 of table 7.3) is shown in figure 7.2 without the uncertainty terms and in figure 7.3 with the uncertainty terms. The improvement in fit is evident throughout.

7.7 CONCLUSIONS

This chapter has developed specifications for and estimated two types of investment equation for plant and machinery expenditure (including leasing) in manufacturing. The first of these is a simple vintage model where the regression was carried out on the levels of the variables and where most of the adjustment process is represented by the lagged dependent variable. A fairly satisfactory equation was obtained which indicated a strong negative role for output growth uncertainty on plant and machinery investment. The estimates were not, however, robust under the addition of terms in profitability, though the negative influence of uncertainty remained significant.

A subsequent section developed an error correction specification, and this was estimated with and without uncertainty terms. The inclusion of terms in growth uncertainty was found to improve the diagnostics considerably, enhancing the explanatory power with acceptable parameter stability. This constitutes fairly strong evidence for a long-run effect of this type of uncertainty on investment. Inflation uncertainty was found to have a short-run influence only.

APPENDIX 7.1:   REPORT ON PRELIMINARY WORK USING THE DISPERSION OF FORECASTS AS AN INDICATOR OF UNCERTAINTY: ANNUAL DATA

The results presented here are for an annual investment study undertaken in the mid 1980s. The definitions of most of the variables used in this study are relatively straightforward and are described in the results section. The only unorthodox series is the uncertainty index. This is derived from a unique record of past forecasts of a number of forecasting teams, extending back to the late 1960s. This information was kindly made available by the Economics and Statistics Division of the National Economic Development Office. It consists of forecasts made by the National Institute for Economic and Social Research, by the OECD and by HM Treasury.

The uncertainty indices are measured as the root mean square deviation, taken each year across three forecasts and calculated separately for each of the variables: real GDP, real investment expenditure and real consumer expenditure. The construction of a normalized index (by dividing by the mean forecast) was rejected lest it lead to spurious correlation when investment is regressed on the indices. Data are also available on inflation forecasts but, owing to restrictions on reporting HM Treasury forecasts of this in earlier years, it was not possible to produce a usable index of this series. So far as possible, the forecasts are all made in the first quarter of the year for the year in question, though there are some exceptions.

The indices of uncertainty are expected to capture the differences between subjective judgements of the modellers. To some extent this will understate the degree of uncertainty that prevails, since forecasts are generally made on the assumption of unchanged policies and there will be occasions in which the continuance of policy is in doubt (e.g. in election years). There is also some doubt as to whether aggregate measures of uncertainty for the whole economy capture the uncertainty felt by individual firms in particular markets. Given that unexpected outcomes will bring not just changes in particular industries but offsetting changes in others, the covariance between individual industry forecasts may be negative, causing the aggregate degree of uncertainty to understate the true index.

Functional form

The construction of the uncertainty indices as described limited the historical span of data from 1969 to 1985, which gave only seventeen observations. The specification of the regression equations has to reflect this limitation; there is a necessity to economize on degrees of freedom. Clark (1979) has shown that the flexible accelerator outperforms most other investment models, so this is taken as the basic functional form, with uncertainty indices and cost of capital as possible additional variables. Some researchers tend to use private GDP and investment on the grounds that government fixed investment may be counter-cyclical, but it is difficult to justify this approach. Private investment will respond to government expenditure, and government investment will, at least partially, respond to government as well as private output. It is thus not sensible to estimate functions using the private sector data only. A rational distributed lag form was adopted, as degrees of freedom are conserved by approximating a high-order lag polynomial by a quotient of two lagged polynomials. The maximum lag investigated was two on the dependent variable I (gross domestic fixed capital formation) and two on the independent variable G (first difference in GDP). These functions were estimated for plant and machinery.

The investment data are measured gross, and researchers normally add a term in the capital stock to capture depreciation. Quite apart from measurement problems, this is a questionable procedure as depreciation and replacement investment will only be well represented by a constant times capital stock when the age structure is constant. Following a period of rapid investment, the age structure is such that although the capital stock may be greatly increased, replacement investment may well be lower for a number of years. For this and for other reasons, the capital stock term has been absorbed into the error term in this study.

Before discussing the result, it is of some interest to see how some particular representations of the rational distributed lag may be justified. One fairly general form allowed for by the lag structure is

$$I_t = A + \alpha I_{t-1} + \beta G_t + \gamma \sum_{i=1}^{\infty} \lambda^{i-1} G_{t-i} + e_t \qquad (7.7)$$

where I is fixed investment and G is first difference in GDP. The presence of the lagged dependent variable indicates the presence of decision and gestation lags; some projects, especially half-completed long-term construction projects, are hard to control, and there are carry-over expenditures in most programmes. The contemporaneous GDP difference is estimated freely, with the remaining terms having a geometrically declining lag scheme.

This permits an inverted-V lag structure. After manipulation, this yields

$$I_t = A + (\lambda + \alpha)I_{t-1} - \alpha\lambda I_{t-2} + \beta G_t + (\gamma - \lambda\beta)G_{t-1}$$
$$+ e_t - e_{t-1} \tag{7.8}$$

There is a non-linear constraint implicit in the coefficients on the I terms, and the error terms is moving average. In the estimation discussed in the following the first restriction was not imposed, but rather the general rational lag form was estimated. If the generalized Koyck scheme with carry-over effects adequately captured the data, an insignificant coefficient on I_{t-2} would indicate short decision and gestation lags. This would be quite likely in the case of plant. An insignificant coefficient on G_{t-2} would indicate an unmodified Koyck scheme with declining weights throughout. Other variables will appear in contemporaneous form in the transformed equation if they enter (7.7) as an infinite series of past observations with a declining weight pattern identical to that on the GDP variable.

Results

The results are presented in table 7.5. In most of the equations, there is little evidence of misspecification indicated by the W (White) or ARCH (Engle) tests, distributed respectively as $\chi^2(m)$ and $\chi^2(1)$. The R^2 and Durbin-Watson figures are highly acceptable. The coefficient on G is stable over a number of specifications, as is its lagged value where entered; both tend to be significant. Lagged investment is highly significant but greater than one, indicating dynamic instability over the sample period, perhaps reflecting the bias towards this type of investment. The negative term for the constant may be contributing to this, but Clark (1979) has defended the expedient of such formulations. Two uncertainty indices were entered in the equations: uncertainty with respect to real GDP (ZO) and the sum (ZZCI) of uncertainty with respect to fixed investment and consumer expenditure. The uncertainty indices are always signed as expected. However, for the specifications shown, ZO is only significant at the 10 per cent level (one-sided test) in equation 1. ZZCI is significant at the 1 per cent level in equation 2 and at 10 per cent in equation 4. In equation 3 ZO

TABLE 7.5 Investment (*I*) equations for UK plant and machinery, all sectors, 1969 to 1985: *t*-statistics in parentheses

Variable	Equation			
	1	*2*	*3*	*4*
Constant	−2.17	−1.88	−2.18	−2.04
	(1.66)	(1.78)	(1.94)	(2.09)
G	0.09	0.08	0.12	0.10
	(2.40)	(2.49)	(3.38)	(3.17)
G(−1)			0.06	0.05
			(2.28)	(1.74)
I(−1)	1.20	1.22	1.16	1.19
	(11.06)	(14.16)	(12.21)	(14.64)
Z	−0.32	−0.15	−0.13	−0.09
	(1.55)[a]	(2.78)[b]	(0.70)	(1.61)[a]
W	11.54(9)	8.27(9)	15.6(14)	16.0(14)
ARCH	2.65	0.00	10.76	3.28
R^2	0.93	0.95	0.95	0.96
DW	1.94	2.23	2.12	2.13

[a] Significant at 10 per cent.
[b] Significant at 1 per cent.

Variables
G   first difference in GDP at constant prices
I   plant and machinery gross domestic fixed capital formation at constant prices
Z   in equations 1 and 3, ZO, uncertainty in respect of real GDP; in equations 2 and 4, ZZCI, sum of uncertainty indices for real consumer expenditure and fixed investment

Diagnostics
W   White test for heteroscedasticity
ARCH   Engle test for antoregressive conditional heteroscedasticity
DW   Durbin-Watson statistic

is not significant, though here the ARCH test is badly failed, suggesting misspecification.

Taken together, these results provide some support for the hypothesis that uncertainty adversely affects investment behaviour for the case of plant.

Finally, the equations in table 7.5 were all rerun using the OECD cost of capital services for the UK in place of the uncertainty indices. In no case was this variable correctly signed. This is not entirely unusual or unexpected in investment equations of this type (Shapiro 1986, p. 163), particularly since the cost of capital was relatively stable over a large part of the estimation period.

APPENDIX 7.2: VARIABLE DEFINITIONS AND DATA SOURCES FOR TABLES 7.2 AND 7.3

The dependent variable is gross domestic fixed capital formation in manufacturing at 1985 prices. The variable has been adjusted to include Bank of England data on leasing, which has been trended upwards over the sample period.

The uncertainty measures are again proxied by the dispersion (standard deviation) of the year-ahead forecasts for output growth and inflation, constructed as in appendix 6.1.

The remaining terms in the regressions are relatively straightforward. The relative price term is a measure of the cost of capital services over the earnings rate. These are both proxies for what ought to be measured. The cost of labour services to the employer will include non-wage labour costs, and the cost of capital should include terms in taxation and capital allowances. The decision to omit the latter was taken on the grounds that the number of competing hypotheses are too large to test in our small sample, where the accent is elsewhere. Thus c/w is represented by $(r - \dot{P} + \hat{\delta})P/w$. The term r is the three-month interbank nominal interest rate. $\dot{P}$ is the rate of inflation for investment goods (manufacturing plant only) and P is the corresponding level. $\hat{\delta}$ is, as described in the text, the rate of depreciation with variable scrapping. The quarterly earnings per person in the whole economy are represented as w; this will move closely with the manufacturing wage rate. The profitability variable is calculated as the net real rate of return for manufacturing industry, as reported in *British Business*.

NOTES

1 A good account of investment equation specification may be found in Precious (1987).

2 For diversified firms, our measures may capture systematic risk and thus be a more accurate proxy for firm uncertainty.

3 In our empirical series of growth and inflation dispersion, the correlation coefficient over the sample of 40 or so observations is 0.18.

4 It is also arguable that price uncertainty may stand for a longer-term indication of demand uncertainty, associated with government reaction to variation in domestic prices.

5 We cannot expect, with our small data set, to discriminate between the many models of uncertainty. For example, although some models suggest an interaction effect between profitability and uncertainty (Nickell 1978, p. 74), that channel may be indistinguishable from the more usual profitability effects, modelled in a log-linear framework.

6 Specifically, YV is often taken in the literature to be $[Y(t) - Y(t - 1) + \delta Y(t - 1)]$, where δ is the rate of decay of capacity (Catinat et al. 1987). We have used a disequilibrium value of δ, $\hat{\delta}$. This is calculated as $\hat{\delta} = \delta[1 + a(re - \overline{re})]$, where re is the percentage of respondents in the CBI *Industrial Trends Survey* giving either replacement or efficiency as a prime reason for new investment, and $\overline{re}$ is the time-averaged mean – over the whole sample – of the same. Thus the disequilibrium value of the scrapping rate moves about the equilibrium value in accordance with survey information. The value of a could be estimated but, given our small sample size, we preferred to impose a value constraining the variation. A value of unity, giving a deviation range of about 30 per cent, was imposed; this is not out of line with such empirical studies as exist, though it may fail to capture the severity of the scrapping in some years. This restriction was tested and easily accepted. The equilibrium value is calculated by the usual formula $\delta = g[(1 + g)^N - 1]^{-1}$, where g is steady state growth of the capital stock, proxied by the growth rate of output, and N is the life of capital equipment.

7 An alternative is that payback periods are shortened.

8 Survey evidence shows that managers are risk-averse for large decisions but risk-neutral for small ones (Aiginger 1987, p. 163). Furthermore, irreversibility applies more to long-lived capital than to non-perishable output, which may be added to inventory.

9 In log-linear specifications, this will imply an interaction effect between profitability and uncertainty.

10 The cost of capital term used in this chapter excludes taxation and capital allowance on the grounds that the variety of ways of measuring the effect of these variables is too great to be taken account of in our small sample. An attempt was made to allow for the taxation changes in the mid 1980s by entering a dummy for 1985 and 1986, when transi-

tion to a new system might have been expected to change the timing of investment. However, this dummy was not significant. Chirinko and Eisner (1983) enter tax variables in a number of investment models and find only modest effects of tax parameter changes on investment. The interest rate used in the levels equation is a long rate (twenty-year gilts). In response to a referee's comment, the short rate was used in the error correction formulation introduced in section 7.6. Both rates give very similar results.

11 It has not been usual to defend this form empirically, and it may appear to conflict with the rectangular lag distribution on authorizations found in Lund et al. (1976). However, that rectangular distribution was found for a specification which involved an AR(2) error. It is not impossible for this to be consistent with the Koyck formulation if the autoregressive error term was due to the omission of lagged actual investment terms.

12 Although the equation was unstable, a strong negative effect on investment from output uncertainty persisted in all specifications.

13 Part of this section draws on Driver and Moreton (1991).

14 Integral control involves a term formed as the summation over i of $[\log I(t - i) - \log YV(t - i - 1)]$. The latter might be justified as reflecting the cumulative evidence available as to whether or not orders are on track. This of course corresponds to actual managerial practice with cusum charts and the like.

15 It is possible to reparameterize the specification with multiple proportional control terms to reflect a distribution on gestation time, but the data did not appear to support a simple formulation of further impact terms on output.

16 The value of 1.96 is suggested by Dolado and Jenkinson (1987), as appropriate for the case where a deterministic trend is present, a feature which finds some support in our series. Our t-statistic for $\log I$ is somewhat above this. When expressed as levels rather than logs, however, both series pass this test also.

17 The t-value obtained in testing the null hypothesis that $h = 1$ was 0.7. Alternatively, the ADFT may be performed by imposing the unity coefficient. In this case the ADFT t-statistics are -2.81, or -3.80 with fifth and sixth lags omitted.

18 For equations 1 and 2 we have reported only the sum of the Almon lag coefficients over the adjustment period. The shape of the Almon lag is similar in both cases, with the coefficients falling gradually from an initial high.

19 The use of Almon lags frequently raises questions in respect of the admissibility of any implicit or explicit restrictions. The lag structures

used here have no end-point constraints imposed. The acceptability of the Almon structure was confirmed by an *F*-test.

20 The results with the inclusion of a long-run inflation uncertainty term are virtually identical to those without it; the fourth lag of the variable had a coefficient of −0.05 and a *t*-statistic of 0.89, when entered in equation 2.

21 For information, it may be noted that the mean and standard deviation of growth uncertainty were 0.67 and 0.27 respectively, while the corresponding figures for inflation uncertainty were 0.92 and 0.31.

8

The Effect of Uncertainty at
Industry Level

8.1 INTRODUCTION

This chapter is concerned with the industry-level response of investment authorizations to variation in uncertainty. The desirability of disaggregation arises partly from the fact that investment behaviour is known to be different in different industrial contexts (Panic and Vernon 1975; Peterson 1976; Sarantis 1979). A second virtue of disaggregation is that it involves industry-level indicators of uncertainty. Industries may operate in an uncertain environment even when broad macro-aggregates are forecast with confidence. Finally, and most importantly, there may be different channels of influence from uncertainty to investment in different industrial contexts.

The broad specification of the investment equations is discussed in section 8.2. Section 8.3 discusses the likely factors behind the differential response to uncertainty across industries. Section 8.4 derives measures of uncertainty at industry level based on business optimism surveys. Section 8.5 discusses the detailed specification of the estimation equations. The results are presented in section 8.6 both for total manufacturing and for industry groups. Section 8.7 discusses the variety of response to uncertainty across industries. The conclusions are noted in section 8.8.

8.2 SPECIFICATION

Before discussing the influence of uncertainty, we will briefly introduce the specification of a basic investment equation.

A common specification is the flexible accelerator derived as an optimal response to adjustment costs. Clark (1979) tested a number of competing models on US data, in particular the flexible accelerator model and a modified neoclassical model where the lag structures on output and relative prices were not constrained to be equal. The results tended to favour the accelerator model, though the discussion supported a role for relative prices. Catinat et al. (1987) found similar results for European countries and also found significance for profitability terms. The latter can be justified either by reference to Tobin's *Q* theory (Clark 1979) or as representing the cost of stockout in an uncertainty model (Malinvaud) 1983). In some studies capacity utilization is used as an additional accelerator model, with the short-term effect modified by the degree of capacity pressure. The latter variable has tended in some periods to be highly correlated with profitability (Panic and Vernon 1975).

The preferred basic specification follows closely those above, with the dependent variable being authorization rather than actual investment. This has the merit of shortening the lag structure. Authorizations for plant and equipment expenditure will be related to change in output; relative factor prices of capital to labour; and capacity utilization. The formal specification is set out in appendix 8.1. One novel feature is that all the data come from the survey questions – the CBI *Industrial Trends Survey*. Appendix 8.2 reports the survey questions used in the estimation.

8.3 THE INFLUENCE OF UNCERTAINTY

There are at least two channels of influence for uncertainty on capital inputs which may be expected to differ in importance across industries. These are the channels of risk aversion and the marginal cost of uncertainty.[1]

Risk aversion is likely to bias downwards the capital input in most cases (see section 4.5.2). Certainly, for a firm with fixed coefficients technology facing an uncertain demand, optimal capacity will always be lower than under certainty for the risk-averse firm (Nickell 1978). Risk aversion is likely to vary across industries, with smaller firms being considerably more risk-averse. Freeman

(1982) confirms this is in a contrast between the chemicals industry and scientific instruments. However, it must be noted that this does not necessarily mean that smaller firms will respond more sensitively to variation in risk. Decision making may be so cautious in the small-firm context that normal variation in risk has little effect. This will be particularly true where the information-gathering capacity of small firms is limited, so that variation in uncertainty may be registered less accurately than for larger firms.[2] The most the theory predicts is that size (as a proxy for risk aversion) should be a discriminant of sensitivity to variation in risk.

The marginal cost of uncertainty model predicts a depressing effect of uncertainty on capital input, where the expected cost due to unsold production dominates. This can be shown to be the case where the profit per unit is less than the unit capital cost, assuming inflexible prices (Nickell 1978, p. 72; Aiginger 1987, p. 84). Clearly the extent to which these conditions apply varies across industries and provides a rationale for observing interindustry variation in response to uncertainty.

The above considerations are for one-shot models in that they relate to optimal capacity rather than to investment. Abstracting from irreversibility constraints, it can be shown that the effect of uncertainty in a dynamic model with delivery lags is to smooth the adjustment (Nickell 1978, p. 103). In this sense the effect of uncertainty is difficult to disentangle from the presence of adjustment costs, and both can give rise to a flexible accelerator response. In the empirical estimation to follow we simply complement the accelerator response by a separate response to uncertainty.

8.4　INDUSTRY-SPECIFIC UNCERTAINTY MEASURES

In establishing a series for industry-level uncertainty we cannot use the same approach as we did for aggregate uncertainty. No reliable and comprehensive set of independent industry-level forecasts is published. Stockbroker forecasts may exist, but to our knowledge there are no long-run series which could be used as a basis for calculating dispersion measures. Accordingly, we have calculated proxies for uncertainty based on differences between firms' expectations of own industry behaviour. These data are contained in the quarterly *Industrial Trends Survey* carried out by the Confederation of British Industry (CBI). We have defined the dispersion across firms in terms of the entropy implicit in the qualitative response given to questions in the form of 'up', 'down' or 'same'. Entropy is defined as $\Sigma [- S_i \log S_i]$, where S_i is the share of each of the three reply categories. When the answers are equally dispersed, E reaches its maximum of $\log 3$ corresponding to maximum uncertainty (Waterson 1984). As actual firm data are kept confidential, there seems no other way of assessing the dispersion across firms in each industry.

We have confined ourselves for the most part to a general measure of uncertainty as recorded by the question on optimism. Specifically this asks whether the firm is more or less optimistic than in the previous four months in respect of the 'general business situation in your industry' (question 1). This is one of the few questions in the survey which refers to the industry rather than the firm, and accordingly the dispersion of the answers is likely to represent differing perceptions of the industry prospects rather than the different conditions faced by individual firms. The term 'optimism' will, of course, be interpreted differently by different respondents, but the use of this question allows the survey response to dictate the emphasis on which dimension of uncertainty is most important at any time.

The entropy measure will not be satisfactory for highly heterogeneous industries. This will apply especially to data for total manufacturing. Accordingly, we have for this case used the aggregate dispersion measures described in chapter 7.[3]

8.5 SPECIFICATION

As discussed in appendix 8.1, the equation to be estimated for each industry has the general form

$$
\begin{aligned}
\text{BAL}(A) = b_0 &+ b_1 \text{ YTERM} + b_2 \text{ CUTERM}(-1) \\
&+ b_3(L)\text{DLCU} + b_4(L)\Delta \log (c/w) \\
&+ b_5 (L) \Delta \log \sigma
\end{aligned}
\tag{8.1}
$$

The dependent variable represents the rate of change of authorizations as proxied by the CBI balance statistic discussed in appendix 8.1. YTERM and CUTERM together capture the accelerator effect. DLCU and Δlog (c/w) refer respectively to differenced log terms in capacity utilization and factor prices.[4] Δlog σ is the term for optimism uncertainty (entropy), again in differenced log form. It is also to be understood that a lagged dependent variable might be justified in some circumstances.

The estimation of (8.1) was carried out using a fairly standard specification for total manufacturing and for each of the individual nine industrial groups. We have allowed different lag structures in the various industries. For the relative price terms we have used an Almon lag structure with no restrictions when it seems that more than two terms may be significant.[5] In keeping with the results of the previous chapter, the lags here are quite long; the data seemed to indicate a minimum initial lag of four.

We have severely limited the choice of lags for the uncertainty variables to avoid the temptation to mine the data. It seems reasonable to suppose that if uncertainty is taken account of in expected authorizations, it will do so contemporaneously or with a very short lag. Accordingly we have allowed a maximum lag of one, and permitted either or both contemporaneous and lagged values to be entered.

8.6 RESULTS

8.6.1 Total manufacturing

Table 8.1 gives the results for a variety of formulations. The first equation in table 8.1 corresponds to (8.5) (see appendix 8.1). The use of a contemporaneous YTERM variable and a single lag on CUTERM was supported by the data. However, the equation is clearly inadequate in that it fails the LM4 test, though none of the LM1, DW or CHOW4 tests indicates any problem. The second equation in the table augments the first with a set of lagged terms in DLCU and in the first difference of relative prices. The *t*-statistics on these additional variables are generally highly significant, and significance is also evident for at least one uncertainty variable discussed in the following. The diagnostics are,

TABLE 8.1 Total manufacturing expected authorizations (BAL (A)): absolute *t*-statistics in parentheses

	Equation	
Variable	1	2
Constant	−91.70 (6.55)	−62.56 (6.05)
YTERM	0.43 (5.58)	0.29 (4.75)
CUTERM(−1)	24.76 (6.25)	16.50 (5.57)
DLCU		33.03 (3.61)
DLCU(−1)		1.39 (0.15)
DLCU(−2)		21.98 (20.81)
DLCU(−3)		24.76 (3.00)
DLCU(−4)		30.61 (3.31)
$\Delta\log (c/w)(−5)$		−4.50 (2.85)
$\Delta\log (c/w)(−6)$		−3.28 (1.93)
$\Delta\log (c/w)(−7)$		−4.49 (2.65)
$\Delta\log \sigma_{\dot{p}}$		−6.63 (2.64)
$\Delta\log \sigma_{\dot{p}}(−1)$		−4.17 (1.50)
$\Delta\log \sigma_g$		−0.98 (0.34)
R^2	0.76	0.96
$\bar{R}^2$	0.74	0.93
DW	1.70	1.93
LM1	0.93 (1,33)	0.01 (1,22)
LM4	3.40 (4,30)	2.72 (4,19)
CHOW4	0.31 (3,31)	0.41 (4,19)

Variables
All balance variables and the entropy variable have been constructed using percentages rather than proportions.

BAL (*A*)	balance of ups over downs in CBI question 3b
YTERM	accelerator term
CUTERM	error correction term in output
DLCU	first difference in log of capacity utilization
c/w	relative price of capital and labour services
$\sigma_{\dot{p}}$	inflation uncertainty: SD across twelve forecasting teams of inflation rate in next twelve months
σ_g	output growth uncertainty: SD across twelve forecasting teams of growth rate in next twelve months

Diagnostics
The diagnostics reported in tables 8.1 to 8.3 are the standard ones produced by Micro-TSP (R^2, $\bar{R}^2$ and Durbin-Watson (DW)) and three additional tests constructed to augment the TSP software. These are Lagrange multiplier tests for autocorrelation of order one (LM1) and four (LM4) and a Chow tests (CHOW4) for structural change obtained by reserving the last four observations for testing for stability. These three test statistics are distributed under the null as F with degrees of freedom given in parentheses.

on balance, more favourable when the expanded variable set is entered, and in particular the LM4 statistic is now acceptable at the 5 per cent level.

We did not expect to get a significant response to the entropy of optimism for the total manufacturing equation, given that this variable will primarily reflect differences in expectations between industries when the individual optimism responses are aggregated as in the total case. We were confirmed in this expectation. The aggregate dispersion measures used in chapter 7 were entered and the results are shown in table 8.1. Inflation uncertainty had a significant short-run negative effect on authorizations with a lag of one and possibly two. No long-run effect could be discerned. Growth dispersion did not seem to have any significant negative effect. Discussion of this is postponed to section 8.7.

8.6.2 *Industry groups*

Table 8.2 gives the results for five out of the nine industry groups estimated where some significance was found for the entropy terms. These industry groups are food, drink and tobacco (FDT); mechanical engineering (ME); electrical and instrument engineering (EIE); other manufacturing (OM); and chemicals (CHEM).

We first describe the general performance of the equations before commenting on the uncertainty terms. In the case of chemicals the data indicated a lag on YTERM but no significance for contemporaneous or lagged changes in capacity. For food, drink and tobacco, no significance could be found for the lagged levels term in capacity utilization; this was omitted because it was signed incorrectly.

In the remaining cases the levels term in capacity utilization was generally highly significant, as were most of the other terms in change in capacity and change in relative prices. The latter were entered as Almon lags where significance was indicated for more than three free lags or where the free lags indicated a pattern but none was significant on its own.

The diagnostics for the equations reported in table 8.2 are generally acceptable, though there are specification problems in the case of both food, drink and tobacco and chemicals, where the CHOW4 tests are failed. On inspection of the residuals, this failure appeared to be due to a higher variance of the error term in the

TABLE 8.2 Disaggregated expected authorizations (BAL (A)): t-statistics in parentheses

Variable	FDT	ME	EIE	OM	CHEM
Constant	0.60	−38.07	−16.89	−71.73	−24.89
	(0.31)	(3.30)	(0.89)	(9.71)	(2.33)
YTERM	0.20	0.29	0.29	0.24	0.22
	(2.44)	(3.68)	(3.42)	(5.90)	2.15)
YTERM (−1)					0.18
					(1.66)
CUTERM (−1)		9.64	6.53	19.34	5.95
		(2.77)	(1.28)	(9.05)	(2.15)
DLCU		37.54		45.06	
		(4.19)		(6.67)	
DLCU (−1)	11.98	35.10		−9.84	
	(1.63)	(3.69)		(1.39)	
DLCU (−2)		41.40		34.65	
		(4.97)		(5.29)	
$\Delta \log (c/w)$ (−4)	A(2,4,7)	A(2,4,7)			
	−6.64	−13.27		−3.54	
	(0.82)	(2.41)		(2.19)	
$\Delta \log \sigma$	−37.25	−129.95	−919.82	−117.55	
	(0.68)	(1.92)	(2.02)	(3.28)	
$\Delta \log \sigma$ (−1)	−86.58		−221.56		−137.08
	(1.56)		(2.28)		(1.63)
R^2	0.34	0.89	0.39	0.94	0.44
$\bar{R}^2$	0.18	0.86	0.29	0.93	0.35
DW	2.01	1.51	1.50	1.90	1.46
LM1	0.04	1.54	2.14	0.02	1.25
	(1,28)	(1,26)	(1,30)	(1,28)	(1,30)
LM4	0.74	0.96	0.48	0.81	1.81
	(4,25)	(4,23)	(4,27)	(4,25)	(4,27)
CHOW4	3.04	0.61	0.80	1.40	3.49
	(4,25)	(4,23)	(4,27)	(4,25)	(4,27)

Variables and diagnostics as for table 8.1, with the addition of the following variable:

σ entropy of optimism in CBI question 1

On relative price c/w, notation A(2,4,7) means second-order Almon lag with no restrictions, starting with lag 4 and ending with lag 7. The coefficient for the sum of the lagged terms is given with its t-value.

last four quarters. No simple respecification suggested itself as necessary to avoid bias in the coefficients.

The diagnostics of the industry equations not reported – those showing no significant effect of uncertainty – were all satisfactory. These industry groups comprise textiles; metal products; metal manufacture; and vehicles. For vehicles, sensible results could only be obtained by entering the lagged dependent variable. It is possible that this group – which includes shipbuilding and aerospace – has such long lags on output that we are merely picking up a long distributed lag effect.

In table 8.2 the change in entropy was entered contemporaneously and with a lag. In each of the reported cases a short-run negative effect of optimism entropy was observed. No lagged level of the entropy term was close to significance, suggesting that there is no long-term effect on authorizations. The strength of significance varied among the groups: one was significant at the 1 per cent level (other manufacturing), one was significant at 2.5 per cent (electrical and instrument engineering), one was significant at 5 per cent (mechanical engineering) and two were significant at 10 per cent (food, drink and tobacco, and chemicals).[6] The remaining four cases (not reported) gave little support to the influence of uncertainty, and in some cases the uncertainty variables were not signed as expected, though none was significantly so.

It was suggested earlier that uncertainty would affect differently the response of different industries. Risk aversion might be strongest in small firms, resulting in a size differential effect in the sensitivity of different industries to variation in uncertainty. Furthermore, the marginal cost of uncertainty effect – operating under inflexible pricing – would work most strongly for firms with low markup in relation to unit capital cost. Flexible pricing, however, may be characteristic of small firms.

Evidence of the strength of these arguments may be assessed using figure 8.1. The horizontal line shows the proportion of employment in enterprises with more than 500 workers. The five industries where a significant uncertainty effect was found are marked by a cross, and the other four by a square.

It is apparent that size of enterprise is a reasonably good discriminator of significance. Except for vehicles – already noted to be unusual in that the lagged dependent variable is doing most

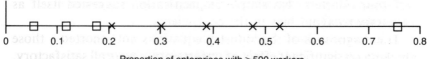

Proportion of enterprises with >500 workers

Industry uncertainty:

✕ Significant

☐ Non-significant

FIGURE 8.1 Industry uncertainty significance and enterprise size: scale shows proportion of employment in enterprises employing more than 500 workers

of the work – all the significant industries are characterized by a greater concentration in large-sized enterprises than the non-significant industries. The lack of a significant uncertainty influence for vehicles could also be due to the heavy state involvement (through subsidies and public purchasing) in the road vehicles, shipbuilding and aerospace sectors that comprise this industry group.

It is not entirely clear why the industries dominated by larger enterprises should exhibit greater sensitivity to uncertainty. One explanation is the more cohesive information-gathering and decision-making capacity. Another possibility is linked with the marginal cost of uncertainty effect discussed earlier. The smaller-enterprise industries are more likely to adjust *ex-post* and thus no marginal cost of uncertainty effect will operate (see Aiginger 1987, p. 96). But it may also simply be that the entropy measure has less random fluctuation in surveys of large firms.

8.7 AUTHORIZATIONS AND INVESTMENT

The results in tables 8.1 and 8.2 contain two puzzles. Firstly, why does there appear to be no long-term effect for the entropy or uncertainty variables? And secondly, why does growth uncertainty not appear to have even a short-run impact on total manufacturing authorizations?

In answering these questions one point seems central. Unlike the decision actually to incur investment expenditure, the decision to authorize expenditure is not irreversible. As Rowley and Trivedi (1975) note in respect of the US Conference Board series on capital appropriations: 'Postponements and outright cancellations are common' (p. 29). It seems likely therefore that by modelling planned authorizations we have only captured one part of the effect of uncertainty on investment. This may explain the lack of a long-run influence for optimism entropy in the industry equations and for dispersion in the total manufacturing case.

For the total manufacturing results in table 8.1, the short-run influence of inflation dispersion observed in chapter 7 was confirmed, though growth uncertainty was not significant. This result again seems likely to reflect the focus on authorizations. The authorization decision will be taken with financial considerations in mind, and inflation uncertainty will feature here. The actual investment decision on the other hand will involve consideration of market risk and irreversibility, and here the growth uncertainty effect should be present. Put differently, if growth uncertainty does not affect authorizations, it should nevertheless affect the response of actual investment to authorizations.

There is a large literature on the modelling of the so-called realization function between actual and intended (authorized) investment (Modigliani and Weingartner 1958; Lund et al. 1976; 1980). To model the process by which intentions are translated into reality we need to know the exact period to which the intentions refer, the price basis most respondents use, data on expected and actual prices, and any other possible determinants of the discrepancy between intended and actual investment, including supply delays and carry-overs from previously authorized investment. In the case of the CBI intentions, the task is made more difficult because the replies are only qualitative and are only translatable into a rate of change rather than a level.

In the equation to be reported here we have not taken account of all the above considerations. Rather we have estimated a rudimentary realization function by regressing the fourth difference of investment (at constant prices) on lagged balances of authorizations from the CBI survey, capacity utilization and a set of uncertainty variables. The capacity utilization variable is included because previous work has suggested that there is a cyclical element in the realization function.[7] In the Department of Industry interview study mentioned above, price changes do not appear to be regarded by interviewees as important in explaining the difference between intention and realization (Lund et al. 1976).[8] To test this, we included a simply proxy for price forecast error – the residual from an AR(2) regression in the log of investment goods prices – but it failed to show up close to significance with any lag. We found it necessary to include a single lag on the dependent variable. The results are shown in table 8.3.

The authorization balance figure is significant with a lag of one. In the first equation of table 8.3 the change in the growth dispersion variable is shown with a lag of two. This is just short of significance at the 5 per cent level in a two-sided test, providing support for the view that output growth uncertainty has its effect in the period between intentions and installation.

Surprisingly, the inflation dispersion term, lagged twice, appears

TABLE 8.3 Investment realization function ($\Delta_4 \log I$) for total manufacturing, 1978(4) to 1987(4): t-statistics in parentheses

	Equation	
Variable	*1*	*2*
Constant	0.25 (1.72)	0.26 (1.91)
$\Delta_4 \log I\,(-1)$	0.53 (5.48)	0.50 (5.45)
BAL $(A)\,(-1)$	0.004 (4.93)	0.005 (5.77)
$\Delta_4 \log \sigma_g\,(-2)$	−0.041 (−2.03)	−0.035 (−1.84)
$\Delta_4 \log \sigma_{\dot{p}}\,(-2)$		0.042 (2.50)
$\log CU\,(-1)$	−0.069 (−1.71)	−0.071 (−1.89)
R^2	0.87	0.89
$\bar{R}^2$	0.85	0.87
DW	2.05	2.20
LM1	0.04 (1,31)	0.48 (1,30)
LM4	1.03 (4,28)	0.51 (4,27)
CHOW4	0.94 (4,28)	0.70 (4,27)

For variables and diagnostics, see table 8.1; CU is defined in appendix 8.1.

significant with a positive sign in the second equation. This seems to be a fairly robust effect. It is present under different specifi- cations, and the inclusion of the variable does not alter the other coefficients greatly. The results from table 8.1 have already indicated that inflation dispersion affects the planned authoriza- tion growth rate with a lag of one or two. Substituting for the lagged authorization balance in table 8.3, the negative influence noted in table 8.1 seems to be roughly cancelled in the period between planned authorization and actual investment. We have been unable to find a significant effect for any levels uncertainty variable in the realization function. This indicates the need for continuing research.

8.8 CONCLUSIONS

Industries dominated by large enterprises are more sensitive to variation in uncertainty. The results may also appear to conflict with the perception of the smaller firm as more risk-averse, but it was noted earlier that small firms may not have the information resources to track uncertainty as closely as larger firms and may therefore be less responsive to variation in uncertainty. Alter- natively, the industrial pattern of response may be due to different competitive conditions.

In this chapter we have looked for evidence that uncertainty affects investment at the stage of planned authorization. In the total manufacturing sample we found a short-run inflation uncertainty effect only. Regression equations were estimated for planned authorization for nine industrial subgroups of total manufacturing. In five of these there was evidence that general uncertainty – as measured by the entropy of the optimism index – was contributing a negative short-run influence to planned authorization.

For the total manufacturing case, a realization function relating actual investment to planned authorizations was estimated. This appeared to indicated that output growth uncertainty had an effect during the realization period. The results also suggest that the negative influence of inflation uncertainty at the stage of planned authorizations may be cancelled at the realization stage.

APPENDIX 8.1: DERIVATION OF AN ACCELERATOR
FORMULATION IN ERROR CORRECTION FORM
FROM CBI SOURCES

One accelerator specification for authorizations A can be written as

$$A = c + b_1 L(\Delta Y)$$

where ΔY is the change in output and L is the lag operator. When this is differenced it yields

$$\Delta A = b_1 \Delta L(\Delta Y) \qquad (8.2)$$

Writing BAL(A); BAL (ΔY) for the balance of ups over downs in the CBI *Industrial Trends Survey* it has been shown that, for the relevant series, balances correspond to first differences (Lund et al. 1976; Rosewell 1985; Pesaran and Wright 1989). Thus we may write (8.2), adding a constant for generality, as

$$\text{BAL}(A) = b_0 + b_1 L(\text{BAL}(\Delta Y)) \qquad (8.3)$$

The independent variable can only be obtained by approximation since the available data are on BAL (Y) and not BAL (ΔY) (survey question 8). So

$$\text{BAL}(\Delta Y) = \Delta \log [Y - Y(-1)]$$

Using the Taylor approximation, we may write this as

$$\Delta \log Y - \Delta[Y(-1)/Y] = \text{BAL}(Y) + \Delta[\{Y - Y(-1)\}/ Y - 1]$$

This may be approximated by BAL$(Y) + \Delta$BAL(Y). Thus the differenced relationship may be written as

$$\text{BAL}(A) = b_0 + b_1[\text{BAL}(Y) + \Delta \text{BAL}(Y)] \qquad (8.4)$$

One problem with this relationship is that if the independent variable is measured with error, as is likely, the coefficient may be severely biased in a downwards direction. A related problem is that the specification ignores any long-run relationship between the levels of the variables.

One solution would be to introduce external data on levels of actual data such as investment and output to proxy the missing variables. We have preferred to stay with the survey data but to construct the required variables from other survey data. The missing variable is an error correction term representing the difference between lagged levels of the dependent and independent variable, i.e. we require data on $(\log A - \log \Delta Y)(-1)$, possibly with further lags on ΔY.

The required term, assuming depreciation to be roughly proportional to the capital stock, may be written as a constant plus $[\log \Delta Y^* - \log \Delta Y]$, where maximum output Y^* is assumed to be proportional to the capital stock. The term in brackets [] may be written as

$$\log[(Y^*/\Delta Y) - (Y^*(-1)/\Delta Y)]$$

Using a Taylor approximation, this becomes

$$\log(Y^*/\Delta Y) - Y^*(-1)/Y^* = \log Y^* - \log \Delta Y$$
$$+ (Y^* - Y^*(-1)/Y^*) - 1$$

Again using the Taylor expansion on $\log \Delta Y$, we can replace it by $\log Y - Y(-1)/Y$. On substitution, the error correction term becomes

$$\log Y^* - \log Y + (Y(-1)/Y) - 1 + \Delta \log Y^*$$
$$= \log (Y^*/Y) - \Delta \log Y + \Delta \log Y^*$$
$$= - \log (CU) - \Delta \log (CU)$$

where CU is capacity utilization Y/Y^*. The advantage of this approximation is that data on CU are available from the survey. CU is taken as unity minus the balance who say that capacity is below a satisfactory level.

Lagging the approximation to the differenced levels, we obtain

$$BAL\,(A) = b_0 + b_1\,[BAL\,(Y) + \Delta BAL\,(Y)]$$
$$+ b_2\,[\log\,(CU) + \Delta \log\,(CU)]\,(-1) \qquad (8.5)$$

where b_2 is expected to be positive. In the text we call the two terms in brackets [] YTERM and CUTERM respectively.

Other terms justified in the text are capacity utilization in differenced log form DLCU, factor prices c/w and entropy σ. The first term is expected to be positive and the latter two negative.

APPENDIX 8.2: CBI INDUSTRIAL TRENDS SURVEY QUESTIONS
USED IN THE TEXT

1 Are you more, or less, optimistic than you were four months
ago about the general business situation in your industry?
3b Do you expect to authorize more or less capital expenditure in
the next twelve months than you authorized in the past twelve
months on plant and machinery?
4 Is your present level of output below capacity (i.e. are you
working below a satisfactory full rate of operation)?
8 Volume of output. Is the trend over the past four months up,
down or same? Is the expected trend over the next four months
up, down or same?

NOTES

1 These are not the only channels; others include 'technological non-
linearities' and the effect of irreversibility of commitment on investor
behaviour (Aiginger 1987; Bernanke 1983). However, these seem less
likely to have identifiable differences in strength across industries.
2 Aiginger (1987) asked survey respondents to choose between a form
of wording which essentially implied expected utility maximization
and an alternative which characterized uncertainty as a state where the
past offers no guide to the future. The replies split fairly evenly, but
the latter characterization was given greater support by small firms.
3 There is some precedent for the use of these industry-specific entropy
measures. Using Austrian data for output growth, Aiginger (1986)
found a reasonably high correlation (0.32) between an aggregate
entropy measure and a cross-section standard deviation across 21
industrial branches for the 80-quarter period from 1964. Thus there
is some support for the belief that entropy can be considered as a
measure of dispersion akin to that used in the previous chapter for
the aggregate investment study. Aiginger also found a correlation
(0.27) between entropy and forecast error as constructed from survey
forecasts.
4 The CBI data contain a number of questions on prices and unit costs,
but none of these is specific enough for us to be able to construct an
industry series on *relative* prices that could be useful in a fixed investment equation. Accordingly, we have chosen to use the aggregate

manufacturing relative price series used in the previous chapter.

5 We have avoided the use of Almon lags for the change in capacity utilization. The combination of the error correction terms in both the level and the rate of change of utilization along with a lagged structure for utilization itself imposes no restriction on the equation if first lag in change in utilization is included. As we tended to find that this first lag was often low in relation to the other terms, we did not want to force it into a constrained pattern as would be the case with the Almon procedure.

6 It may seem surprising that the highest significance is found for a seemingly heterogeneous industry – other manufacturing. However, that industry is largely dominated by paper products and intermediate inputs.

7 This may partly be due to supply considerations. Discrepancies between the Department of Industry investment intentions and actual out-turns of investment have been shown in interview studies to be influenced by supply constraints to an important extent. Certainly the empirical work reported by Lind and other suggests a role for the level of investment relative to its trend, perhaps proxying supply factors. This again suggests the inclusion of capacity utilization.

8 This might indicate that, during the period surveyed, either price expectations were generally correct or absolute price changes are responded to with an elasticity of unity, an assumption that involves the rather implausible implication of no contingency reserve for investment.

9

Conclusions and Implications
of the Research

9.1 INTRODUCTION

We have now addressed the main issues set out in the introductory
chapter, namely the central role of fixed investment in economic
growth and the adverse effect of uncertainty on investment.

This chapter briefly summarizes the main arguments and
findings of the book in sections 9.2 and 9.3. The general policy
implications are set out in section 9.4. The book ends by stressing
the importance of the results and noting some specific implications.

9.2 THE MAIN ARGUMENTS SUMMARIZED

In very long-run equilibrium, variation in investment shares should
not affect the growth rate of the economy. But this must immediately be qualified by noting, firstly, that investment can boost
growth for a considerable transitory period; and secondly, that
this can become permanent through the operation of virtuous or
vicious cycles that characterize trading economies. Although the
focus of the book is on fixed investment, many of the arguments
here apply with equal force to any future commitment – especially
those that are long-lived and irreversible such as R&D or
training.[1]

Uncertainty tends to have an adverse effect on investment. The
variety of possible economic models should not obscure the fact
that the most important channels of influence centre either on risk
aversion or on the irreversible nature of the commitment. The

theory has been discussed in chapter 4. In most realistic contexts demand uncertainty, operating through these channels, will depress investment.

A focus on long-term commitments such as fixed investment is especially important in a context of capital shortage. This may be the case in countries such as the UK where investment orientation is excessively short term for institutional reasons. The problem here is especially acute in sectors of the economy with greatest irreversibility – production industries. In this climate of short-termism the effect of increased uncertainty can be severe.

Economies in the process of structural change are especially vulnerable to uncertainty. It is at such times that opportunities are greatest in new markets. But uncertainty and structural change are correlated, implying that uncertainty is most likely when it is most damaging.

9.3 THE MAIN EMPIRICAL FINDINGS SUMMARIZED

Empirical testing requires that we address the measurement problems involved in quantifying uncertainty. We have proposed and used the cross-section dispersion of forecasts. The intuitive reasoning is clear and attractive. High interpersonal variation will reflect high (average) personal uncertainty. This intuition was supported with theoretical and empirical arguments in chapter 5. The econometrics of chapter 6 demonstrated that cross-forecast variation encapsulated other measures of uncertainty more often used in the literature, such as volatility, conditional volatility or forecast error.

The main empirical findings on the effect of uncertainty on total manufacturing have been presented in chapter 7. The most important points are that uncertainty matters and that it is output growth uncertainty that has been shown to have a significant – and permanent – depressing effect on investment. The long-run effect is moderate, but this is almost certainly an underestimate since no account is taken of the effect of uncertainty on output and, through output, on investment. Furthermore there may be a tendency for uncertainty to bias the fixed investment decision towards shorter asset lives, which would blunt the effect of uncertainty on plant and machinery purchases.

The material in chapter 8 showed an adverse effect of uncertainty in respect of business optimism on planned investment authorization. The focus on authorization rather than expenditure may have resulted in observing only a short-run effect at industry level. A similar short-run effect – for inflation uncertainty – was observed for total manufacturing planned authorizations. This appeared to be reversed during the realization phase as authorizations were translated into expenditure. A further negative effect for output growth uncertainty was also observed during the realization phase, suggesting that cancellation or postponement of plans is the route by which growth uncertainty affects investment.

9.4 GENERAL POLICY IMPLICATIONS

The notion that uncertainty depresses economic growth is not new. As Meltzer (1989) has argued, it is *the* central point of Keynes' *General Theory*. Most schools of economic thought will accept the aim of reduced uncertainty, though some will follow the Knightian or Austrian tradition of seeing uncertainty as a spur to entrepreneurial activity. For the remainder, there is a dichotomy between those who see the market as self-regulating and those who follow a disequilibrium approach. Equilibrium economists call for simple non-discretionary rules as the best environment for market equilibrium to prevail in the face of shocks. Their opponents argue for a range of interventionist measures, perhaps to reduce uncertainty (indicative planning) or to compensate for uncertainty (stabilization policy). We consider these measures in turn.

9.4.1 Indicative Planning

This involves direct provision of information not provided by market mechanisms, backed up by effective methods to make the associated forecasts credible. The aim is reduced uncertainty. This cannot normally be achieved by increased information alone but requires an agent to enforce an outcome or at least to ensure the likely conditions for the outcome.[2] Planning has merits and demerits and it is difficult to argue a *general* case for or against (Richardson 1990).

Of the many arguments against indicative planning, the one with most force seems to be that government does not know any better than industry what the future holds.[3] This may be true or false, but the conclusion drawn as to the irrelevance of government targets is not valid when uncertainty is known to depress activity. Commitment to a growth target reduces risk to the firm; it effectively insures private investors against risk. Since this will increase growth, expected growth under government insurance will be higher than without it; recall that it is growth uncertainty that depresses investment. Assuming that the government can manipulate short- to medium-term growth, it will be able to offer a credible target growth rate higher than the average private expectation because the credible target will lessen uncertainty and risk.[4] However, it should be clear that the process is not costless for any growth target. The cost to the government of being able to offer this credible growth target is the loss of flexibility and increased variability in regard to other target variables, e.g. inflation. Our results indicate, however, that inflation uncertainty does not appear to hinder long-run capital growth.[5]

9.4.2   *Stabilization Policy*

Stabilization policies are pursued to counter business cycle fluctuations in output. The above discussion has not supported the usual dichotomy between indicative planning and stabilization policy (Black 1968). The two approaches seem to be connected in that stabilization is necessary to make forecasts credible. There is econometric evidence to the effect that some stabilization policy has been counter-productive in the past (Artus et al. 1981). On the other hand, stabilization rules automatically related to the business cycle seem to have had some success. The automatic stabilizers in the economy include the taxation system, which damps the volatility of private expenditure. Investment reserve funds, whereby investment funds are creamed off during the boom to be released during the downturn, appear to lead to a more stable investment cycle (NEDO 1978; Taylor 1982). A mechanism such as this could be particularly important for countering growth uncertainty when it seems to be strongest – at times of negative growth at the bottom of the cycle.[6] The same applies to any self-financing tax/subsidy scheme for promoting investment. Stability of investment could also be promoted by institutional reforms to discourage 'short-termism', and possibly by increased 'networking' agreements between companies.

9.5 THE IMPORTANCE OF THE FINDINGS AND SPECIFIC IMPLICATIONS

The importance of the econometric results lies in the establishment of a tradeoff between output uncertainty and growth. The dominant concern in the macroeconomic literature – when uncertainty is given any attention – is the tradeoff between inflation uncertainty and growth (Ball and Cecchetti 1990). This has not been established in our study. Macroeconomists frequently justify deflationary policies to reduce the level of inflation and hence long-run inflation uncertainty, which is held to be costly. Our results do not give backing to this, since the costs of uncertainty for growth appear to derive – via investment at any rate – from growth uncertainty.

Some specific implications of our study are set out in conclusion as follows. Firstly, we have shown that uncertainty depresses investment. This in itself is destructive of much of the economic theory, which argues that all demand management is ineffective. The policy ineffectiveness result is derived for rational expectations models where risk has no effect.[7] Secondly, we have shown that it is output uncertainty that depresses investment. This implies that policies to reduce this uncertainty could have a payoff in faster growth. Targets for attainable growth could credibly reduce uncertainty at a cost of some flexibility in regard to other targets. Thirdly, we have argued that the quantification of the uncertainty effect which we have provided can be used to inform stabilization policy and make that policy more effective. Finally, a further implication follows from a consideration of the relationship of growth uncertainty with the economic cycle. It was shown in chapter 6 that growth uncertainty tends to be unusually high when growth is negative, i.e. at the bottom of the cycle. Thus there may be a particular case for uncertainty reducing policies at this point.

NOTES

1 R&D is, however, distinctive in that part of its function is to reduce uncertainty.

2 Black (1968) proposes an approach which will 'stabilize the economy by creating a stable pattern of expectations rather than by manipulating demand by monetary and fiscal policies after disturbances have already occurred' (p. 309). The latter may, however, be necessary in order to produce the hoped-for stability of expectations.

3 Of course this does not mean that it could not obtain such information; Keynes once suggested the publication, enforced by law, of all business data. Leontief (1985) recounts how large US corporations such as Bechtel and Arthur D. Little have libraries of information on input–output statistics which would be useful in national economic forecasting.

4 The danger that this will override the rational caution of individual investors is lessened by noting that, in contrast to risk-averse individuals, society can avoid the borrower's and lender's risk of default.

5 Inflation uncertainty may, of course, have other welfare effects. Adverse effects may also be more severe outside the normal range for developed economies.

6 NEDO (1978) pointed to the difficulties in introducing the Swedish approach because of the prevailing UK first-year capital allowances. In the introduction to that report, Lord Roll noted that 'tax relief for an investment reserve might be relevant in Britain if the tax regime were to change at some time in the future'. Of course, the system has changed in exactly the direction indicated.

7 Begg (1983) remarks that 'individuals may care, not just about the mean of future random variables, but also about other measures of their statistical distribution' (p. 263).

References

Abel, A.B. 1983: Optimal investment under uncertainty. *American Economic Review*, 73, 228–33.

Aiginger, K. 1986: Alternative empirical measures for the degree of uncertainty. In K.H. Oppenlander and G. Poser (eds), *Business Cycle Surveys in the Assessment of Economic Activity*, Aldershot: Gower.

Aiginger, K. 1987: *Production and Decision Theory under Uncertainty*. Oxford: Basil Blackwell.

Arestis, P. and Skuse, F. 1989: Austerity policies and the new right: recent UK experience. Mimeo, Polytechnic of East London.

Arrow, K.J. 1962: The economic implications of learning by doing. *Review of Economic Studies*, 29, 155–73.

Arrow, K.J. 1984: Alternative approaches to the theory of choice in risk-taking situations. In K.J. Arrow, *Individual Choice under Certainty and Uncertainty* (collected papers), Oxford: Basil Blackwell.

Artis, M.J. 1982: Why do forecasts differ? Paper 17, Panel of Academic Consultants, Bank of England.

Artus, P., Muet, P.A., Palinkas, P. and Pauly, P. 1981: Economic policy and private investment since the oil crisis: comparative study of France and Germany, *European Economic Review*, 16, 7–51.

Artus, P. and Muet, P.A. 1990: *Investment and Factor Demand*. Amsterdam: North-Holland.

Baldwin, R. 1989: The growth effects of 1992. *Economic Policy*, October, 247–83.

Ball, L. and Cecchetti, S.G. 1990: Inflation and uncertainty at short and long horizons. *Brookings Papers on Economic Activity*, 1, 215–54.

Banerjee, A., et al. 1986: Exploring equilibrium relationships in econometrics through static models: some Monte Carlo evidence. *Oxford Bulletin of Economics and Statistics*. August, 253–78.

Batchelor, R.A. 1985: Inflation uncertainty: theory and measurement for the European economy. Paper presented to the CIRET Conference,

162   *References*

Vienna.
Batchelor, R.A. and Orr, A.B. 1987: Relative price dispersion, variability and credibility as determinants of inflation uncertainty. Discussion Paper 61, City University Business School, London.
Bean, C. 1981: An econometric model of manufacturing investment in the UK. *Economic Journal*, March, 91–121.
Bean, C. 1989: Capital shortage. *Economic Policy*, April, 11–54.
Begg, D. 1983: *The Rational Expectations Revolution in Macro-economics: theory and evidence*. London: Philip Allan.
Bernanke, B.S. 1983: Irreversibility, uncertainty and cyclical investment. *Southern Economic Journal*, February, 85–106.
Black, J. 1968: The theory of indicative planning. *Oxford Economic Papers*, 20, 303–19.
Blanchard, O. and Dornbusch, R. 1983: US deficits, the dollar and Europe. In O. Blanchard, R. Dornbusch and R. Layard (eds), *Restoring Europe's Prosperity*, London: MIT Press.
Bombach, G. 1985: Post-war economic growth revisited. *Professor Dr. F. de Vries Lectures in Economics: theory, institutions, policy*, vol. 6, Amsterdam: North-Holland.
Bosworth, D. 1988: Capital stock, capital usage and supply-side constraints. In *Institute for Employment Research Annual Review*, Warwick University, chapter 3.
Caballero, R.J. 1991: On the sign of the investment–uncertainty relationship. *American Economic Review*, 81, 279–88.
Carvalho, F.J. Cardim de 1988: Keynes on probability, uncertainty and decision making. *Journal of Post-Keynesian Economics*, 11, 1, 67–81.
Catinat, M., Cawley, R., Ilzkovitz, F., Italianer, A. and Mors, M. 1987: The determinants of investment. *European Economy*, 31.
Chick, V. 1983: *Macroeconomics after Keynes: a reconsideration of The General Theory*. Oxford: Philip Allan.
Chirinko, R.S. and Eisner, R. 1983: Tax policy and investment in major US macroeconometric models. *Journal of Public Economics*, 20, 139–66.
Clark, P. 1979: Investment in the 1970s: theory, performance and prediction. *Brookings Papers on Economic Activity*, 1, 73–113.
Coddington, A. 1982: Deficient foresight: a troublesome theme in Keynesian economics. *American Economic Review*, 72, 3, 480–7.
Davidson, P. 1991: Is probability theory relevant for uncertainty? A post-Keynesian perspective. *Journal of Economic Perspectives*, 5, 1, 129–43.
Davis, J.B. 1989: Keynes on atomism and organicism. *Economic*

Journal, 99, 1159–72.

Dickey, D.A. and Fuller, W.A. 1981: The likelihood ratio statistic for autoregressive time series with a unit root. *Econometrica*, 49, 1057–72.

Dixon, H. 1986: Strategic investment with consistent conjectures. In D.J. Morris et al. (eds), *Strategic Behaviour and Industrial Competition*, Oxford: Clarendon.

Dolado, J.J. and Jenkinson, T.J. 1987: Cointegration: a survey of recent developments. Oxford Applied Economics Discussion Paper 39, Oxford University.

Domberger, S. 1980: Managers, market structure and the rate of price adjustment. In K. Cowling et al. (eds), *Mergers and Economic Performance*, Cambridge: Cambridge University Press.

Driffill, J., et al. 1989: Costs of inflation. Discussion Paper 293, Centre for Economic Policy Research, London.

Driver, C. 1986: The scrapping behaviour of concentrated and non-concentrated industries in the UK. *Applied Economics*, 18, 249–63.

Driver, C. 1987: *Towards Full Employment: a policy appraisal*. London: Routledge.

Driver, C. 1989: Measuring the loss of the industrial capital stock. *Royal Bank of Scotland Review*, September, 27–32.

Driver, C. 1990: Structural change in UK manufacturing 1975–85. *Applied Economics*, October.

Driver, C. 1991: Measuring the pace of structural change in the UK economy. In C. Driver and P. Dunne (eds), *Structural Change in the UK Economy*, Cambridge: Cambridge University Press.

Driver, C. 1992: Rethinking Heiner's reliability condition. *American Economic Review*, March.

Driver, C. and Dunne, P. (eds) 1991: *Structural Change in the UK Economy*. Cambridge: Cambridge University Press.

Driver, C., Lambert, P. and Vial, S. 1991: Risky production with *ex-ante* prices. Mimeo, Management School, Imperial College, forthcoming in *Bulletin of Economic Research*.

Driver, C. and Moreton, D. 1991: The influence of uncertainty on UK manufacturing investment. *Economic Journal*, November.

Eichner, A.S. 1976: *The Megacorp and Oligopoly*. Cambridge: Cambridge University Press.

Eliasson, G. 1984: The microfoundations of industry policy. In A. Jacquemin (ed.) *European Industry, Public Policy and Corporate Strategy*, Oxford: Oxford University Press.

Eliasson, G. and Fries, H. (eds) 1983: *Microeconomics*. Yearbook of the Industrial Institute for Economic and Social Research, Stockholm.

Eltis, W. 1966: *Economic Growth: analysis and policy*. London: Hutchinson.

Ergas, H. 1984: Corporate strategies in transition. In A. Jacquemin (ed.), *European Industry, Public Policy and Corporate Strategy*, Oxford: Oxford University Press.

Ford, J. L. 1983: *Choice, Expectations and Uncertainty*. Oxford: Martin Robertson.

Foster, R. 1986: *Innovation: the attacker's advantage*. London: Pan.

Freeman, C. 1982: *The Economics of Industrial Innovation*. London: Printer.

Freeman, C. 1985: *Technological Trends and Employment vol. 4. Engineering and Vehicles*. Aldershot: Gower.

Freeman, C. and Soete, L. (eds) 1987: *Technical Change and Full Employment*. Oxford: Basil Blackwell.

Ghemawat, P. 1984: Capacity expansion in the titanium dioxide industry. *Journal of Industrial Economics*, 33, 2, 145–63.

Gilbert, R. J. and Lieberman, M. 1987: Investment and coordination in oligopolistic industries. *Rand Journal of Economics*, 18, 17–33.

Gillies, D. A. 1973: *An Objective Theory of Probability*. London: Methuen.

Gold, B. 1979: *Productivity, Technology and Capital*. Lexington, MA: Lexington Books.

Gosling, S. 1986: Effects of exchange rate volatility on UK exports. Economic Working Paper 24, National Economic Development Office, London.

Gowdy, J. 1985–6: Rational expectations and predictability. *Journal of Post-Keynesian Economics*, 8, 2, 192–9.

Granger, C. W. 1986: Developments in the study of cointegrated economic variables. *Oxford Bulletin of Economics and Statistics*, 48, 3, 213–28.

Hacche, G. 1979: *The Theory of Economic Growth*. London: Macmillan.

Hamouda, O. F. and Smithin, J. N. 1988: Some remarks on 'Uncertainty and economic analysis'. *Economic Journal*, 98, 159–64.

Harcourt, G. C. 1972: *Some Cambridge Controversies in the Theory of Capital*. Cambridge: Cambridge University Press.

Hartman, R. 1976: Factor demand with output price uncertainty. *American Economic Review*, 66, 4, 675–81.

Hay, D. A. and Morris, D. J. 1991: *Industrial Economics and Organisation: Theory and Evidence*. Oxford: Oxford University Press.

Heiner, R. 1983: The origin of predictable behaviour. *American Economic Review*, September, 560–95.

Heiner, R. 1985a: Predictable behaviour: reply. *American Economic Review*, June, 579–85.

Heiner, R. 1985b: Origin of predictable behaviour: further modelling and applications. *American Economic Review*, May, 391–6.

Heiner, R. 1985–6: Rational expectations when agents imperfectly use information. *Journal of Post-Keynesian Economics*, 8, 2, 201–7.

Heiner, R. 1986: Uncertainty, signal-detection experiments, and modelling behaviour. In R. Langlois (ed.), *Economics as a Process*, Cambridge: Cambridge University Press.

Heiner, R. 1988: Imperfect decisions and routinised production: implications for evolutionary modelling and inertial technical change. In G. Dosi et al. (eds), *Technical Change and Economic Theory*, London: Pinter.

Hey, J.D. 1979: *Uncertainty in Microeconomics*. Oxford: Martin Robertson.

Hey, J.D. 1981: *Economics in Disequilibrium*. Oxford: Martin Robertson.

Hey, J.D. 1983: Whither uncertainty? *Economic Journal*, 1982 Conference Papers, 130–9.

Hogg, R.V. and Craig, A.T. 1971: *Introduction to Mathematical Statistics*. London: Macmillan.

Hull, J.C. 1980: *The evaluation of risk in business investment*. Oxford: Pergamon.

Hunter, J. and Pescetto, G. 1991: Structural economic change and manufacturing investment in the UK. In C. Driver and P. Dunne (eds), *Structural Change in the UK Economy*, Cambridge: Cambridge University Press.

Jefferson, M. 1983: Economic uncertainty and business decision making. In J. Wiseman (ed.), *Beyond Positive Economics*, Proceedings of Section F (Economics) of the British Association for the Advancement of Science, New York: St Martin's.

Junankar, S. 1989: How companies respond to the Industrial Trends Survey. Paper presented to the CBI conference, London, 6 November.

Kaldor, N. and Mirrlees, J.A. 1962: A new model of economic growth. *Review of Economic Studies*, 29, 174–90. Reprinted in A. Sen (ed.) 1970, *Growth Economics: selected readings*, Harmondsworth: Penguin, 343–66.

Karlin, S. and Carr, S. 1962: Prices and optimal inventory policy. In Arrow et al., *Studies in Applied Probability and Management Science*, Stanford: Stanford University Press, 159–72.

Kendall, M.G. 1973: *Time Series*. London: Griffin.

Kennedy, P. 1985: *A Guide to Econometrics*. London: Basil Blackwell.

Keynes, J.M. 1973: *The Collected Writings of John Maynard Keynes. Vol. VI: A Treatise on Money - 2 The Applied Theory of Money. Vol. VII: The General Theory. Vol. VIII: A Treatise on Probability. Vol. IX: Essays in Persuasion. Vol. XIV: The General Theory and After, Part II*. London: Macmillan.

Kindleberger, C.P. 1967: *Europe's Postwar Growth: the role of labour supply*. Cambridge, MA: Harvard University Press.

King, M.A. 1972: Taxation and investment incentives in a vintage investment model. *Journal of Public Economics*, 1, 121–47.

Klau, F. 1984: Comments. In R. Layard, S. Nickell and P. Jackman, Unemployment, real wages and aggregate demand in Europe, Japan and the US, CLE Paper 214, London School of Economics.

Knight, F.H. 1971: *Risk, Uncertainty and Profit*. Chicago: University of Chicago Press.

Kon, Y. 1983: Capital input choice under price uncertainty: a putty-clay technology case. *International Economic Review*, 24, 4, 183–97.

Koutsoyiannis, A. 1983: *Non-Price Decisions: the firm in a modern context*. London: Macmillan.

Lambert, J.P. and Mulkay, B. 1987: Investment in a disequilibrium context, or does profitability really matter?. *Cahier du Cerec*, 870, Bruxelles.

Lawson, T. 1985: Uncertainty and economic analysis. *Economic Journal*, 95, 909–27.

Lawson, T. 1987: The relative/absolute nature of knowledge and economic analysis. *Economic Journal*, 97, 951–70.

Lawson, T. 1988: Probability and uncertainty in economic analysis. *Journal of Post-Keynesian Economics*, 11, 1, 38–69.

Leontief, W. 1985: Why economies need input–output analysis. *Challenge*. March, 27–35.

LeRoy, S.F. and Singell, L.D. Jr 1987: Knight on risk and uncertainty. *Journal of Political Economy*, 95, 2, 394–406.

Lindley, D.V. 1965: *Introduction to Probability and Statistics from a Bayesian Viewpoint*. Cambridge: Cambridge University Press.

Lund, P.J., Martin, W.E. and Bennett, A. 1980: Price Expectations and their role in the analysis of the UK Department of Industry's investment intentions inquiries. *Journal of Industrial Economics*, March, 225–39.

Lund, P.J., Meliss, C.L. and Hamilton, V.J. 1976: *Investment Intentions, Authorisations and Expenditures*. London: HMSO.

Lutz, F. and Lutz, V. 1951: *The Theory of Investment of the Firm*. New Work: Greenwood.

Malerba, F. 1985: Demand structure and technological change: the case of the European semiconductor industry. Paper given to EARIE Conference, Cambridge, September.

Malinvaud, E. 1977: *Profitability and Unemployment*. Cambridge: Cambridge University Press.

Malinvaud, E. 1982: Wages and unemployment. *Economic Journal*, 92, 1-44.

Malinvaud, E. 1983: Profitability and investment facing uncertain demand. Working Paper 8303, INSEE.

Mankiw, N.G. 1986: The term structure of interest rates revisited. *Brookings Papers on Economic Activity*, 1, 61-109.

Martin, W. and O'Connor, M. 1981: Profitability: a background paper. In W. Martin (ed.), *The Economics of the Profits Crisis*, London: HMSO.

Mascaro, A. and Meltzer, A.H. 1983: Long- and short-term interest rates in a risky world. *Journal of Monetary Economics*, 12, 485-518.

Matthews, R., Feinstein, C.H. and Odling-Smee, J.C. 1982: *British Economic Growth 1856-1973*. Oxford: Clarendon.

Mayer, C. and Alexander, I. 1990: Banks and securities markets: corporate financing in Germany and the UK. Discussion Paper, Centre for Economic Policy Research, London.

Mayer, T. 1989: Policy simulations with econometric models. *Methodus*, December, 13-14.

McCracken, P. et al. 1977: *Towards Full Employment and Price Stability*. Paris: OECD.

McEachern, W. and Romeo, A. 1978: Stockholder control, uncertainty and the allocation of resources to research and development. *Journal of Industrial Economics*, 27, 1-12.

McHugh, R. and Lane, J. 1987: The role of embodied technological change in the decline of labour productivity. *Southern Economic Journal*, 53, 915-23.

Meltzer, A.H. 1989: *Keynes's Monetary Theory*. Cambridge: Cambridge University Press.

Mendis, L. and Muellbauer, J. 1984: British manufacturing productivity 1955-83: measurement problems, oil shocks and Thatcher effects. Discussion Paper 32, Centre for Economic Policy Research, London.

Michl, T. (1985) International comparisons of productivity growth: Verdoorn's law revisited. *Journal of Post Keynesian Economics*, 7, 474-492.

Modigliani, I. and Weingartner, H.M. 1958: Forecasting uses of anticipatory data for investment and sales. *Quarterly Journal of Economics*, 72, 23-54.

NEDC 1987: *Capacity and Investment*. Annex to NEDC 87 (37). London: National Economic Development Office.

NEDO 1978: *Investment Reserve Schemes*. London: National Economic Development Office.

NEDO 1982: The City and the financing of manufacturing industry's investment. Internal study, National Economic Development Office.

NEDO 1986: Pilot study of corporate investment practice. Internal study, National Economic Development Office, London.

Newell, A. 1984: Annual indices of the changes in the structure of employment by industry and region. Working paper 617, London School of Economics.

Nickell, S.J. 1978: *The Investment Decision of Firms*. Cambridge: Cambridge University Press.

Nickell, S.J. and Wadhwani, S. 1987: Myopia, the dividend puzzle and share prices. Discussion Paper 155, Centre for Economic Policy Research, London.

Nordhaus, W. 1982: Economic policy in the face of declining productivity growth. *European Economic Review*, 131-57.

Norman, J.M. 1975: *Elementary Dynamic Programming*. London: Arnold.

Northcott, J. and Walling, A. 1988: *Impact of Microelectronics: diffusion, benefits and problems*. London: Policy Studies Institute.

O'Driscoll, G. and Rizzo, M. 1985: *The Economics of Time and Ignorance*. Oxford: Basil Blackwell.

Pagan, A. and Ullah, A. 1986: The econometric analysis of models with risk terms. Discussion paper 127, Centre for Economic Policy Research. London.

Panic, M. and Vernon, K. 1975: Major factors behind investment decisions in British manufacturing industry. *Oxford Bulletin of Economics and Statistics*, 37, 191-210.

Paraskevopoulos, D. et al. 1991: Robust capacity planning under uncertainty. *Management Science*, 37, 787-800.

Pesaran, B. and Wright, C.B. 1989: Using and assessing CBI data at the Bank of England. Paper presented to the CBI conference, London, 6 November.

Peterson, W. 1976: Investment. In T. Barker (ed.), *Economic Structure and Policy with applications to the British Economy*, London: Chapman and Hall, chapter 5.

Phillips, L.D. 1975: *Bayesian Statistics for Social Scientists*. London: Nelson.

Pike, R.H. 1982: *Capital Budgeting in the 1980s*. London: Institute of Cost and Management Accountants.

Pindyck, R.S. 1988: Irreversible investment, capacity choice and the value of the firm. *American Economic Review*, 78, 969–85.

Pleeter, S. and Horowitz, I. 1974: The implications of uncertainty for firm and market behaviour. *Metroeconomica*, 24, 181–93.

Porter, M.E. 1983: The technological dimension of corporate strategy. In R. Rosenbloom (ed.), *Research in Technological Innovation, Management and Policy*, vol. 1, Greenwich, CT: JAI Press, 15–33.

Porter, M.E. 1989: *The Competitive Advantage of Nations*. London: Collier Macmillan.

Porter, M.E. and Spence, M. 1981: The capacity expansion process in a growing oligopoly: the case of wet corn milling. In J. McCall (ed.), *The Economics of Information and Uncertainty*, Chicago: University of Chicago Press, 259–316.

Precious, M. 1987: *Rational Expectations, Non-Market Clearing and Investment Theory*. Oxford: Clarendon.

Reimann, B.C. 1990: Why bother with risk adjusted hurdle rates? *Journal of Long Range Planning*, 23, 57–65.

Richardson, G.B. 1990: *Information and Investment: a study in the working of the competitive economy*, Oxford: Clarendon.

Robinson, B. and Wade, K. 1985: Unemployment, scrapping and factor prices. *Economic Outlook Forecast Release*, 9, 10, London Business School.

Robinson, J.V. 1962: *Essays in the Theory of Economic Growth*, London: Macmillan.

Rockley, L.E. 1973: *Investment for Profitability*. London: Business Books.

Romer, P. 1986: Increasing returns and long-run growth. *Journal of Political Economy*, 94, 1002–37.

Romer, P. 1990: Endogenous technological change. *Journal of Political Economy*, 98, s71–s101.

Rosewell, B. 1985: The CBI Industrial Trends Survey and capacity and capacity working. Internal paper, Confederation of British Industry, London.

Rothschild, M. and Stiglitz, J. 1971: Increasing risk: its economic consequences. *Journal of Economic Theory*, 3, 1, 66–82.

Rowley, J.C.R. and Trivedi, P.K. 1975: *Econometrics of Investment*. London: Wiley.

Rowthorn, B. 1989: The Thatcher revolution. *Economic Papers*, 8, 2, 1–22.

Salmon, M. 1982: Error correction mechanisms. *Economic Journal*, 92, 615–29.

Sarantis, N. 1978: Investment stability and industrial structure in UK manufacturing. *Kyklos*, 31, 437–61.

Sarantis, N. 1979: Relative prices, investment incentives, cash flow and vintage investment functions for UK manufacturing industries. *European Economic Review*, 12, 203–25.

Sargan, J.D. and Bhargava, A. 1983: Testing residuals from least squares regression for being generated by the Gaussian random walk. *Econometrica*, 51, 153–74.

Sawyer, M. 1985: *The Economics of Industries and Firms*. London: Croom Helm.

Scherer, F. 1980: *Industrial Market Structure and Economic Performance*. Chicago: Rand McNally.

Scherer, F. 1986: *Innovation and Growth*. London: MIT Press.

Schmalensee, R. 1988: Industrial economics: an overview. *Economic Journal*, 98, 643–81.

Schultze, C. 1987: Savings, investment and profitability in Europe. In R. Lawrence and C. Schultze (eds), *Barriers to European Growth: a transatlantic view*, Brookings, 509–39.

Sen, A. (ed.) 1970: *Growth Economics: Selected Readings*. Harmondsworth: Penguin.

Shackle, G.L.S. 1969: *Decision, Order and Time in Human Affairs*. Cambridge: Cambridge University Press.

Shapiro, M.D. 1986: Investment, output and the cost of capital. *Brookings Papers on Economic Activity*, 1, 111–64.

Simon, H. 1979: Rational decision making in business organizations. *American Economic Review*, 69, 4, 493–513.

Skouras, T. 1982: On economic methodology, or Satan at work. *British Review of Economic Issues*, 4, 114–25.

Smith, A.D. 1987: A current cost accounting measure of Britain's stock of equipment. *National Institute Economic Review*, 120, 42–57.

Soete, L. (ed.) 1985: *Technological Trends and Employment. Vol 3: Electronics and Communications*. Aldershot: Gower.

Spence, M. 1979: Investment strategy and growth in a new market. *Bell Journal of Economics*, 10, 1–19.

Sugden, R. 1987: New developments in the theory of choice under uncertainty. In J.D. Hey and P.J. Lambert (eds), *Surveys in the Economics of Uncertainty*, Oxford: Basil Blackwell.

Taggart, R. 1983: Capital allocation in multi-division firms: hurdle rates vs. budgets. Working Paper. 1213, National Bureau of Economic Research, Cambridge, MA.

Taylor, J.B. 1982: The Swedish investment funds system as a stabilization policy rule. *Brookings Papers on Economic Activity*, 1, 57–105.

Taylor, M. 1987: What do investment managers know? An empirical study of practitioners' predictions. Internal report, Bank of England.

Tirole, J. 1989: *The Theory of Industrial Organization*. Cambridge, MA: MIT Press.

Wadhwani, S. 1987: The effects of inflation and real wages on employment. *Economica*, 54, 21–40.

Wadhwani, S. and Wall, M. 1986: The UK capital stock – new estimates of premature scrapping. *Oxford Review of Economic Policy*, 2, 3, 44–55.

Waterson, M. 1984: *The Economic Theory of the Industry*. Cambridge: Cambridge University Press.

Winslow, E.G. 1989: Organic interdependence, uncertainty and economic analysis. *Economic Journal*, 99, 1173–82.

Woods, M. et al. 1985: Appraising investment in new technology: the approach in practice. *Management Accounting*, 63, 42–3.

Wren-Lewis, S. 1985: The quantification of survey data on expectations. *National Institute Economic Review*, 113, 39–49.

Zarnowitz, V. and Lambros, L. A. 1987: Consensus and uncertainty in economic prediction. *Journal of Political Economy*, 95, 3, 591–621.

Author Index

Author Index

Subject Index